# Mastering Business Excellence

## Secrets to Win in Today's Market

**SIMON MALCOM**

## Contents

Introduction ..................................................................................... 4

Chapter 1: Understanding Business Excellence ................. 7

    The Nine Principles of Excellence ...................................... 13

Chapter 2: Strategic Vision and Planning ........................... 23

    The Importance of a Vision for Scaling Your Business ................................................................................................ 24

    Strategic planning frameworks and methodologies . 30

    Aligning business goals with market demands and trends .................................................................................. 53

Chapter 3: Leadership and Organizational Culture ......... 57

    The Power of Leadership in Shaping Organizational Culture ................................................................................. 58

    How to Create a Continuous Improvement Culture? 63

    Building and nurturing high-performance teams ...... 70

    What are the roles in a high performance team? ........ 76

Chapter 4: Operational Excellence ........................................ 87

    Implementing lean and agile practices ...................... 120

Quality management and performance metrics........128

Chapter 5: Customer Focus and Market Positioning ..134

How to recognize your clients' wishes?........................136

10 Strategies for enhancing customer experience ..140

Mastering Brand Differentiation and Positioning Strategy ................................................................................151

Types of Brand Differentiation Strategies....................157

Conclusion ...........................................................................165

# Introduction

In present day fiercely competitive business landscape, groups face a myriad of challenges and possibilities that form their techniques and outline their achievement. Globalization has intensified opposition, with groups from different corners of the sector vying for market proportion and customer interest. The digital revolution has democratized get admission to markets, enabling startups and established companies alike to disrupt conventional industries with revolutionary technologies and business fashions.

Moreover, the speedy tempo of technological development has shortened product lifecycles, forcing businesses to always innovate to live relevant. In this dynamic surroundings, expertise competitor conduct and marketplace developments is vital for growing effective techniques. Companies have to not handiest reveal direct competitors but also maintain a watch on oblique threats and rising traits that would affect their market role. Strategic making plans, therefore, plays a pivotal position in navigating this competitive landscape, supporting companies count on demanding situations, capitalize on possibilities, and preserve a sustainable aggressive gain.

As agencies strive to differentiate themselves and capture market percentage, agility, innovation, and purchaser-centricity turn out to be key drivers of fulfillment. Embracing virtual transformation, fostering a subculture of continuous mastering and adaptation, and forging strategic partnerships are vital techniques for thriving in brand new competitive business panorama.

Mastering business excellence in state-of-the-art marketplace isn't just high quality however vital for long-time period fulfillment and sustainability. In a globalized and unexpectedly evolving business surroundings, where competition is fierce and consumer expectations are better than ever, agencies that excel in each aspect in their operations have a enormous edge.

Business excellence encompasses a selection of things, consisting of operational efficiency, innovation, consumer pride, and strategic agility. Companies that prioritize excellence in those areas not only meet however regularly exceed market expectancies, fostering customer loyalty and riding sales boom.

Moreover, in a generation ruled by way of virtual transformation and disruptive technology, getting to know business excellence enables businesses to adapt speedy to changes, seize new possibilities, and mitigate risks efficaciously. It also cultivates a culture of non-stop improvement and innovation in the organization, fostering worker engagement and attracting pinnacle skills. Beyond operational benefits, reaching enterprise excellence complements emblem popularity and credibility, setting up a competitive gain this is tough for competitors to replicate.

Ultimately, gaining knowledge of business excellence is not just a goal but a adventure—a dedication to non-stop learning, edition, and innovation that positions agencies as leaders of their industries and paves the way for sustained growth and profitability in today's dynamic marketplace.

# Chapter 1: Understanding Business Excellence

Business Excellence is defined simply as: An incorporated series of tested practices for the way a business ought to function to emerge as the quality it can possibly be – i.e. International class.

It is relevant to all groups whether or not private or public, for-earnings or no longer-for-income and small or big. Of path it yields enormous internet economic advantages.

Business Excellence entails enhancing patron outcomes and increasing productivity through the organization's key techniques and is driven with the aid of organizational leadership and control.

More than just some other "buzz word", business excellence underpins any a hit agency's strategy and boom.

If you need to take your business productivity and growth to new heights, you'll want to implement a practical framework and demonstrated technique for commercial enterprise excellence.

Despite the Simple Definition, the Confusion for SMEs / SMBs is Understandable

Other famous collections of demonstrated practices encouraged during the last 70 years consist of World Competitive Manufacturing, Just In Time, Best Practice, Total Quality Management (TQM), Six Sigma, Agile, Business Improvement, Process Improvement, Business Transformation and Lean Thinking. All of those overlap substantially with each different, and match in the umbrella term 'Business Excellence'. These are all partial solutions, not a complete solution for any enterprise wishing to end up the first-rate it could in all likelihood be within the shortest possible timeframe and at the bottom viable cost.

Not tremendously, CEOs of SMEs / SMBs can get harassed as to which methodology and language they need to adopt.

Even within Business Excellence there are slight variations around the sector regarding the essential criteria for fulfillment. For example, Singapore, Australia and the USA promote 7-eight assessment criteria for Business Excellence, while the Europeans sell nine criteria.

Common Core of Business Excellence globally

Fortunately, all of the eighty or so lively national Frameworks / Models have a commonplace core.

This middle may be summarized as five logical and noteworthy Prerequisites for SMEs / SMBs searching for a realistic implementation method that is easy to recognize. Not relatively, the overriding driver of all five

Prerequisites (see underneath) is Customer Delight for both inner and outside clients.

Process Design & Improvement
Shared Strategic Direction
Performance Measurement & Feedback
Knowledge Capture & Leverage
Leadership & Management of Change

Implementation of these Prerequisites inside the proper order maximizes the return on funding. It gets rid of the possibility of fake starts off evolved and poorly targeted efforts. To keep away from an awful lot wasted effort, it is critical for those Prerequisites to end up completely integrated with admire to every other as their implementation progresses.

Business excellence models have developed considerably through the years, reflecting converting paradigms in management theory and practice. One of the earliest influential models turned into Total Quality Management (TQM), which emerged within the mid-20th century, specially associated with the paintings of W. Edwards Deming and Joseph M. Juran. TQM emphasized non-stop improvement, consumer awareness, and employee involvement as key pillars for reaching excellence in organizational performance. It marked a shift from excellent control to a proactive nice management method, aiming to beautify typical organizational effectiveness.

In the 1980s and 1990s, the Baldrige Excellence Framework won prominence in the United States. Named after Malcolm Baldrige, a former Secretary of Commerce, this framework extended the scope of commercial enterprise excellence past first-class to include broader organizational overall performance criteria consisting of leadership, strategic making plans, purchaser and marketplace consciousness, statistics control, workforce awareness, manner management, and commercial enterprise consequences. This holistic approach advocated groups to evaluate themselves in opposition to rigorous standards, fostering a subculture of non-stop development and innovation.

Simultaneously, the European Foundation for Quality Management (EFQM) introduced the EFQM Excellence Model in the late 1980s. Initially designed for European corporations, this model emphasized comparable standards of TQM however brought dimensions like societal duty and sustainable improvement. The EFQM model additionally included management, approach, people, partnerships, sources, procedures, and patron consequences into a comprehensive framework for attaining excellence. Its flexible shape allowed companies across various sectors and geographies to evolve and practice its concepts effectively.

In the early 21st century, the idea of business excellence multiplied in addition with the upward push of frameworks including Six Sigma, Lean Management, and Agile methodologies. Six Sigma, pioneered through Motorola and popularized by way of General Electric under Jack Welch, focused on decreasing defects and variability in strategies, thereby improving quality and customer satisfaction. Lean Management, derived from Toyota's production gadget, aimed at removing waste and optimizing efficiency across operations. Agile methodologies, to begin with developed for software program improvement, prioritized flexibility, collaboration, and speedy response to change.

Today, business excellence fashions maintain to adapt in reaction to globalization, virtual transformation, and sustainability imperatives. New frameworks emphasize adaptive management, virtual innovation, sustainability practices, and stakeholder engagement as critical factors of organizational excellence. As companies navigate more and more complicated and competitive landscapes, the evolution of those models underscores their enduring relevance in fostering organizational resilience, innovation, and long-time period fulfillment in a dynamic international financial system.

## The Nine Principles of Excellence

Our position as advisers to Privately Held Businesses over many years has given us the opportunity to discover the motives why a few organizations are a long way greater a hit than others.

The following are the "Nine Principles of Excellence" that we use to assist guide private corporations and their leaders on the direction to growth.

Vision

Planning

Values/Culture

Customer Focus

Competitive Advantage

Involve and Empower People

Systems Thinking

Execution

Leadership

Let me touch on every Principle under:

**Vision**

A Vision can wager be defined as a mental and verbal photograph of the preferred future. We call it, thinking about the "result in thoughts".

In our discussions with many owners and leaders of commercial enterprise, we have found that the ones leaders that have a clean vision of what they want the business to be in the destiny are more likely to obtain achievement and meet the preferred results. However, whilst we begin asking the managers in the commercial enterprise we forever discover that the imaginative and prescient has no longer been communicated for the duration of the company.

Part of the problem stems from the reality that while the proprietor has a vision of their mind they are unable, or discover it tough, to talk that imaginative and prescient to their personnel.

Successful businesses but make sure all employees are clean on what the vision and course of the commercial enterprise is. It gives idea to the company and enables become aware of, for his or her human beings, how they match in and make a contribution to the larger photograph.

**Planning**

Successful organizations recognize the importance of running on the commercial enterprise instead of in the business. Planning is the procedure that enables them to work on the commercial enterprise.

Successful people and enterprises recognize that with out a plan, your existence or commercial enterprise is directionless. Without a plan of what you want to achieve there's no innovative tension to do something unique from what you're currently doing.

**Values/Culture**

Values are something which can be crucial to you to your existence. They can in all likelihood quality be defined as an "enduring perception". They guide your decision making technique, no matter whether or not you're consciously aware of your values or now not.

Values are extraordinarily crucial to discuss inside the commercial enterprise context as enterprise choices are primarily based on values. If a business has not mentioned with its key people the values it regards as crucial, then every person action is primarily based at the character's non-public values. The result of this may be that there is no consistency wherein every key employee responds to the same vital problem.

Successful corporations have certainly diagnosed values that are lived and practiced throughout the employer. The value device creates a robust way of life inside the company which provides all new personnel with a clean message of "the manner we do things round right here". This approach that new personnel are quickly indoctrinated through the manner things are done and the manner human beings act instead of simply words on a page.

**Customer awareness**

Understanding what customers need, now and within the future, affects the enterprise route and method of a commercial enterprise.

Successful businesses focus at the wishes of the purchaser as opposed to adopting a product focus. Businesses that concentrate on customer's needs are more likely to expand new services and products to satisfy changing or rising desires in their customers and are higher prepared for change as consumer's needs adjust.

There are many examples in history of organizations that have failed due to the fact they adopted a product recognition believing the services or products could preserve to meet a selected need forever, but, with the creation of new technology their product has become obsolete (Sony, Nokia, Kodak to name some).

**Competitive benefit**

For lengthy-term success a business must differentiate itself from others to ensure patron loyalty. In short, the commercial enterprise has to be able to provide the client something special.

Any business approach, to be able to sustained achievement, ought to be primarily based on a competitive advantage. A competitive benefit is gained whilst a commercial enterprise actions right into a position in which it has an aspect in coping with competitive forces and in attracting customers.

A commercial enterprise, with the aid of coming across and promoting their competitive benefit, can increase their sales, enlarge their client base and enhance their profitability.

Successful enterprises display a clear and tangible competitive gain this is known through their purchaser base.

Unfortunately, in our revel in loads of groups do not try and decide how they might acquire a aggressive advantage and as a end result they merely get through.

**Involve and empower people**

The capability of any business is realized thru its humans' enthusiasm, resourcefulness and involvement.

Successful agencies involve and empower people via:

Ensuring they're concerned inside the method;
Ensuring they may be clear on the direction of the business and the values the enterprise stands for;
Providing exquisite training; and
Providing incentives
Systems wondering

Successful corporations depend strongly on systems to make sure the enterprise operates efficaciously. Success may be duplicated whilst the structures are in area to make sure each worker knows what is anticipated of them.

An vital part of the fulfillment of a commercial enterprise is also pushed by the "records structures" in area. In order to reap excellence an agency needs that allows you to objectively determine its modern-day reputation as well as music its development toward the goals that it has set. i.e. Measure the critical matters.

A key problem of many businesses is the shortage of formal structures and tactics to make certain the business operates correctly and constantly. People troubles tend to be greater in those businesses as employees do no longer understand what's expected of them.

A not unusual trouble amongst non-public groups is that the fulfillment of the commercial enterprise is often heavily reliant at the owner. Without the business proprietor the enterprise would conflict to live to tell the tale. The price of those groups are much less as there aren't any structures and procedures in region to make sure the commercial enterprise can retain while offered.

**Execution**

An execution subculture is important to the success of a commercial enterprise - a Vision and Plan will no longer be realized without motion.

Only while execution is the everyday, will continuous development will become 2d nature.

In our experience failure to execute is the only important that prevents a "top" enterprise becoming "terrific".

**Leadership**

The final Principle of Excellence is leadership. Successful companies all have sturdy leadership. Leaders of a hit organizations deliver truly the imaginative and prescient of the organization and its values and exercise the Nine Principles of Excellence.

A leader of a hit corporations surely acts as the maestro of the orchestra - making sure all the parts of the business are working collectively and successfully.

The chief ensures the involvement of all key employees in the planning procedure and action is taken at the decisions that are made and the motion plans that are advanced.

The Nine Principles of Excellence are essential truths in commercial enterprise that we're all aware about but want to hold the front of thoughts.

# Chapter 2: Strategic Vision and Planning

Having a clean strategic vision is crucial for any commercial enterprise trying to grow and scale efficiently, and when well-described, it acts as a north big name, presenting path and alignment to your company's priorities and efforts.

Without a clear imaginative and prescient, growth can grow to be haphazard and scattershot, main to wasted time and sources. So, taking time to craft an inspirational but manageable imaginative and prescient is a essential exercise for any management crew aiming to take their company to the next level.

## The Importance of a Vision for Scaling Your Business

A strategic imaginative and prescient that clearly articulates your company's destiny function presents numerous blessings:

It gives long-time period course and attention - With a clear vision, personnel understand what you are constructing toward and can align their efforts. Research indicates corporations with engaged personnel develop revenues 2.5x quicker.

It evokes and rallies your crew - An bold imaginative and prescient receives humans enthusiastic about the future and their position in developing it. This results in higher motivation and overall performance.

It allows powerful decision-making - Every key decision may be evaluated on whether or not it advances your vision. This prevents scope creep and wasted resources.

It attracts funding and talent - Investors and pinnacle applicants want to be part of an formidable assignment. Your vision tells them who you are and in which you are headed.

Without a clean imaginative and prescient, it is smooth to get sidetracked through brief-time period wins or glittering objects. Crafting a compelling imaginative and prescient prevents this glide and maintains anybody rowing in the identical path throughout increase.

**Key Elements of an Effective Strategic Vision**

An impactful strategic imaginative and prescient includes four key components:

**Mission** - Your enterprise's middle cause and cause for present. It boils the problem you resolve down right into a simple assertion.

**Values** - The guiding principles and behaviours that shape your lifestyle. These act because the "constitution" for selection-making.

**Vision** - An aspirational description of your favored future nation. Where you are headed and what you wish to attain.

**Goals** - Specific, measurable objectives to consciousness your efforts and benchmark progress closer to the imaginative and prescient. Goals have to be tied to metrics and timeframes.

Getting these factors proper is vital to crafting a vision that resonates and affords powerful route. Companies like Disney, Nike and Apple have built billion-greenback manufacturers on the lower back of their compelling strategic visions.

**Tips for Crafting Your Strategic Vision**

Crafting a vision calls for time and deep questioning. It has to be advanced collaboratively by related to key stakeholders which includes your team, board and traders. Here are a few pointers for developing and refining your imaginative and prescient:

Imagine a formidable destiny - Set sights high. Envision what 10x increase ought to look like in your enterprise. Connect to better reason - Articulate the way you enhance lives and empower human beings through your paintings. This builds engagement.

Keep it simple - Boil down every detail to a sentence or short paragraph. It must be memorable and tweetable.

Make it inspirational - Build excitement and perception. People want to feel your imaginative and prescient is plausible.

Involve others - Get input from the group, customers, and board individuals to decorate imaginative and prescient.

Revisit it often - Review the vision each 6-365 days as your agency evolves.

**Aligning Operations with Your Vision**

Once crafted, the imaginative and prescient should permeate all factors of operations. Here are some first-rate practices:

Cascade your imaginative and prescient into department desires and OKRs. Ensure they ladder up into your vision and support the business' international objectives and route.

Reference the vision when comparing choices, techniques and opportunities. The very simple query to invite is, "will this pass us closer to our imaginative and prescient?"

Weave the vision into enterprise conferences, off sites and materials to reinforce it.

Celebrate wins and milestones that advance you toward your vision. Recognize those contributions; they are vital.

Revisit your imaginative and prescient periodically and adjust it, if wished, as market situations evolve.

Communicating Your Vision for Buy-In

For your vision to take keep, you have to speak it relentlessly thru:

Website, displays, posters - Share imaginative and prescient prominently throughout channels.

Team meetings and networking possibilities - Regularly talk vision and organization direction.

Onboarding and training - Educate employees at the imaginative and prescient from day one.

Lead by way of example - Embody the imaginative and prescient to your phrases, decisions and movements.

Solicit comments - Ensure vision resonates with employees and stakeholders. Refine it if wanted.

## Adapting Your Vision As Your Company Scales

While a strategic vision offers lengthy-term route, it isn't set in stone, and nor ought to its. As your corporation grows and evolves, you may need to make changes whilst keeping its essence.

Review the imaginative and prescient every 6-twelve months during strategic making plans. Update it if wished.

Balance pragmatism with ambition. Set your attractions excessive however ensure they remain conceivable.
Maintain consistency to your mission and values. Evolve the imaginative and prescient and goals as priorities shift.

Engage the team when refining the imaginative and prescient. Ensure it keeps resonating across the organization.

Celebrate updates to the strategic vision as necessary milestones, not failures. Be positive to talk adjustments certainly.

By dedicating sufficient effort and time to carefully crafting and correctly communicating a clear strategic imaginative and prescient, you could successfully align your company for sustainable and scalable boom, making sure long-time period fulfillment. This complete imaginative and prescient, acting because the bedrock for all destiny activities, serves as a guiding light, providing the necessary path and consciousness to construct something truly excellent. While the vision may evidently evolve through the years, keeping a regular and unwavering dedication to its middle concepts will lay the groundwork for attaining exquisite consequences.

Feel unfastened to e-mail me or connect on LinkedIn to hold the verbal exchange, I'd like to help you toward attaining greatness!

## Strategic planning frameworks and methodologies

The great approach management methodologies include Balanced Scorecards (BSC), Objectives Key Results (OKR), Management via Objectives (MBO),

Objective-Goals-Strategies-Measures (OGSM), Scenario strategic making plans, and Blue Ocean method, and they have many similarities.

They assist connect the strategy elements logically and systematically, increasing method alignment and communication with managers and employees. These strategic planning fashions additionally help music and monitor approach execution.

Strategic planning is asking into the destiny and figuring out strategies to obtain business desires. It includes assessing the cutting-edge scenario, developing targets, creating motion plans, and identifying sources. Each strategic making plans version has its specific method to this manner.

If we evaluate the primary factors of all of the maximum-used strategic making plans models, that is what we get:

BSC: Objective > Measures > Initiatives
OKR: Objective > Key Results (Key Results include quantifiable goals)

OGSM: Objective > Goals > Strategies > Measures (Strategies covers tasks)

MBO: Objective (Objective monitored with measures and quantifiable objectives)

Scenario Strategic Planning: Scenario > Strategy (Strategy covers objectives, goals, and initiatives)

Blue Ocean Strategy: Market analysis> Creating a new area precise from competitors

In this submit, we're going to explain the principles of every strategic planning method, their pros and cons, and actual-world examples of businesses the usage of them.

Types of strategic making plans methodologies

Analyzing, growing, and tracking techniques is crucial for any business. Strategic planning frameworks make this clean via allowing business shareholders to set desires, create actionable plans, and track their performance.

Traditional making plans methodologies are the most extensively used and include Balanced Scorecards, Objectives Key Results (OKR), Management by means of

Objectives (MBO), Objective-Goals-Strategies-Measures (OGSM), and Scenario Strategic Planning.

Traditional strategic making plans frameworks cognizance on expertise your situation and putting manageable business desires and goals. These making plans models are still famous due to the fact they permit companies to live updated on their progress.

The following are the maximum not unusual conventional planning methodologies:

**1. The Balanced Scorecard (BSC)**

This overall performance control device facilitates groups measure and display progress towards organizational goals. The Balanced Scorecard higher positions you to assign precedence to their initiatives, song dreams, and measure performance.

The BSC is a simple strategic planning version that gives a complete technique to dealing with the commercial enterprise method with the aid of thinking about quantitative (financial) and qualitative (non-financial) performance measures. It additionally guarantees personnel understand their roles in achieving organizational goals and targets.

BSC links objectives and tasks (or initiatives) to measure performance from four balanced views. These key areas make your business overall performance measurable and less complicated to screen and control. They encompass:

**Financial attitude**

Is your organization earning a go back on its investments? Every business pursuit to achieve profitability even as managing the dangers related to strolling a commercial enterprise. Achieving these goals calls for you to be aware of the financials of your commercial enterprise, inclusive of sales, price, and profit.

A commercial enterprise's financial metrics can also encompass fee of go back, annual budgeted sales and price goals, and earnings statements. These metrics assist measure the employer's financial performance over the years and allow higher decision-making.

## Customer perspective

This entity measures how your business meets consumer needs and the way satisfied customers are along with your products or services. The customer metrics in this entity may additionally encompass customer loyalty, wide variety of court cases, retention price, and Net Promoter Score®.

The Balanced Scorecard compares your business's popularity in your competition. It identifies how to enhance customer pride and differentiates it from the opposition. Some of the methods you may correctly decorate your popularity are thru customer service, advertising, and consumer revel in tasks.

## Business procedure

How your business methods perform is key to attaining your client and monetary dreams? Processes are the building blocks of any company; without effective management, they are able to emerge as inefficient or, worse, useless.

Process metrics can consist of procedure cycle time, value in step with output unit, shipping instances, variety of defects, and nice requirements. Monitoring your planning manner overall performance will help you discover areas for improvement and maximize performance.

**Learning & increase angle**

This attitude makes a specialty of the human beings within your company. It identifies the vital talents, understanding, and capabilities to align them with organizational dreams.

Learning & Growth metrics encompass employee engagement scores, training, and improvement applications, go back on investment in getting to know initiatives, and worker pride surveys.

These metrics help your commercial enterprise broaden the important programs to assist their companies prevail. They are better placed to improve their worker engagement and retention packages.

The Balanced Scorecard (BSC) combines parts of the method, which includes milestones and challenge crowning glory, in place of OKRs focusing on operational efforts and results. Companies that use the BSC admire its typical technique to method.

BSC makes a specialty of pinnacle-down management styles, that is counterintuitive for younger businesses and some industries.

Companies use the Balanced Scorecard to maintain music of their operational and financial metrics. Banks are best examples of industries that rely on data and performance metrics to live beforehand.

Banks ought to display their loan volumes, delinquency, profitability objectives, and deposit growth. They touch clients for remarks and use this records to measure patron pride, lawsuits decision time, and retention rates.

Other metrics banks music the usage of the Balanced Scorecard encompasses worker education hours, manner cycle time, and terminated debts.

The Balanced Scorecard makes strategic planning less complicated through supplying a platform in which corporations can measure and song development in the direction of their goals.

Manufacturing agencies also use BSC to monitor manufacturing quantity, protection facts, and device downtime. These metrics help shareholders make higher choices that assure the agency's stability.

They additionally track financial metrics including fee goals, profits statements, and pricing strategies. Keeping music of those metrics will assist the organization pick out improvement regions and increase its strategic planning model.

The Balanced Scoreboard lets in groups to prioritize their dreams and targets through placing a clean route. This framework ensures your commercial enterprise maximizes on to be had sources to reap the commonplace goal.

BSC also allows you pick out regions that require development to remain productive and aggressive.

The best downside to this pinnacle-down method is that small companies may additionally find it difficult to put into effect it. It is high priced and time-consuming. BSC will also be misguided while measuring patron loyalty and employee pride.

## 2. Objectives and key outcomes (OKRs)

OKR is a aim-pushed strategic planning version this is regularly used to manual and reveal final results-based fulfillment. Using effects instead of obligations as drivers, OKRs inspire duty in reaching achievement via signs.

OKRs are hierarchical. Employees set their desires and progress upward via the ranks. The idea is that when personnel obtain their goals, then managers achieve theirs from the lowest up.

**OKRs are damaged down into two parts:**

**Objectives**
Objectives are the concrete; measurable goals you want to achieve. They give your agency a clean aim to attempt for and make clear what you want to do. You ought to

have a maximum of three objectives for every OKR, which should be challenging but manageable.

**Key results**

Achieving objectives depends on key results, pinpointing measurable results indicating fulfillment. Typically, every objective is connected to three-five key outcomes. Knowing those effects empowers employees to live on course and take ownership of their responsibilities.

The OKR technique establishes three to 5 dreams and assigns them the identical goals.

Software improvement groups especially undertake OKRs to screen their initiatives. Their goals may include decreasing insects, growing new updates, or growing consumer engagement.

They ruin down those targets into the key affects you need to attain to accomplish them. These key effects include time-to-market, customer delight ratings, and Trojan horse reviews.

Other businesses, inclusive of huge retail shops or production agencies, use OKRs to song the performance in their making plans technique. They may additionally set objectives which include reducing transport instances, increasing performance in manufacturing techniques, or enhancing customer support.

OKRs offer a effective framework that aligns your organization's goals with every individual's objectives. By putting clear objectives and key results, your crew can higher degree development and live on track. With OKRs, teamwork turns into even greater critical, encouraging collaboration in the direction of a shared success.

Leveling up your organization's targets and key outcomes (OKR) requires serious dedication. The setup, monitoring, and adjustments should be performed right. Plus, measuring achievement or failure is tricky considering the fact that some desires are subjective and hard to quantify.

Additionally, if the OKR isn't always well communicated or understood, it could lead to confusion and frustration.

### 3. Objective-Goals-Strategies-Measures (OGSM)

OGSM is a international-elegance older strategic planning version that transforms goals, dreams, strategies, and measures into actionable and executable plans. OGSM brings alignment, transparency of priorities, and metrics that define achievement. This framework frames the enterprise's desires and the way it will get there.

OGSM defines fulfillment and facilitates corporation's paintings collectively across functions, geographies, and up and down the line. "Strategies" in OGSM manual the work sports (projects) and allocation of constrained assets throughout the company.

The 4 elements that comprise OGSM make this making plans model comprehensive and effective. They consist of:

**Objectives**

Your long-term visions outline the goals of your strategic plan. Objectives need to be clean, plausible, and measurable. They will offer the overall direction of what you need to accomplish and have to be revisited periodically.

**Goals**

Focus on the "who, what, whilst" of strategic making plans by way of setting clear dreams. Determine who needs to do what and with the aid of whilst to accomplish your enterprise's targets.

**Strategies**

Unlocking your strategic plan's full capacity lies in a hit strategy. These are concrete steps designed to strength your tasks and sports, in the long run bringing you toward your preferred goals.

**Measures**

Measures offer treasured metrics to assess in case you're assembly your dreams and goals. Keeping tabs on your achievement guarantees you are on route and equips you with insights for future selections.

The OGSM is a basic model that offers a complete approach to strategic planning, empowering you to outline objectives, set dreams, create techniques, and music development. Aligning your aspirations with actionable plans permits you to effectively reap your vision and degree your development.

The OGSM making plans model is applicable to a couple of industries, including healthcare and production. It can help map out set objectives and strategies and offer perception for project improvement.

OGSM is a framework manufacturing industries use to set production goals and develop strategies to maximize productiveness. Technology companies can also use it to degree advertising objectives and different essential metrics.

OGSM gives a complete method to a strategic planning technique. It facilitates team's awareness on achieving goals by way of making knowledgeable selections.

The OGSM framework can recognition too much on long-time period objectives and dreams, making it tough to regulate short-term strategies. You may even need strategic making plans tools that make monitoring progress and adjusting techniques clean.

### four. Management by Objectives (MBO)

MBO ambitions to enhance business enterprise performance via defining goals to which management and employees agree. The concept encourages objective setting and participation.

In addition, it creates a degree of commitment on behalf of the personnel, which motivates them more. Most companies that deploy MBO-style overall performance management evaluation their performance annually.

Objectives (and related measures and objectives) are set at the start of the 12 months and then evaluated at the cease. Objectives have a tendency to be vast and strategic versus centered and tactical.

MBO usually follows the mnemonic SMART – Specific, Measurable, Achievable, Relevant, and Time-sure.

MBO can practice to any organization or enterprise. It's generally used within the provider area, in which it may be used to set dreams for purchaser satisfaction rankings and income targets. It can also be used inside the tech enterprise, in which it is able to be employed to set objectives for product improvement and innovation.

MBO creates transparency among control and personnel as goals are agreed on together. It enables increase a sense of ownership amongst all parties involved.

It also helps to create a sense of responsibility among employees. Everyone is aware of the desires and expectations that must be met, and there's a clear path for measuring success.

The MBO model prioritizes dreams and targets, sidelining worker improvement and motivation. The technique creates a high-pressure, aggressive environment as opposed to promoting collaboration.

Stressed employees will do something it takes to meet their goals, even if that means resorting to unethical moves out of worry. This can result in taking shortcuts that in the long run damage the agency's productiveness.

## five. Scenario strategic planning

To prepare for the destiny, a enterprise have to examine the capability effect of moving financial and technological tendencies. This assessment, referred to as state of affairs strategic making plans, facilitates understand and apprehend the opportunities that lie beforehand.

Having a glimpse of the destiny permits you to devise consequently for each situation. This strategic plan includes 4 steps, inclusive of:

**Identify key drivers**

Maximizing your enterprise's productiveness starts off evolved with recognizing how monetary, technological, and business changes can affect your dreams. Discover how each of these factors can have an effect on your company's achievement.

**Come up with the most likely state of affairs**
Discover key tendencies impacting your business enterprise via analyzing accumulated records. Focus on people with the maximum huge impact.

**Develop a strategy for every state of affairs**
Boost your possibilities of achievement with the aid of strategizing for each feasible scenario. Be prepared to modify your technique, framework, or strategies consequently.

**Implement and reveal**
Maximize the fulfillment of your plan by executing it successfully. Craft a clean roadmap to guide your crew in enforcing strategies and monitoring their progress. Ensure each person understands how to research information and pivot for superior consequences.

If you're a farmer, you know the way unpredictable the weather can be and the way it is able to effect your earnings. Scenario making plans facilitates you analyze current weather patterns and other factors to prepare to your next harvest and make knowledgeable decisions about future investments.

Military establishments additionally use this planning version to expect the outcome of operations and plan for any not likely situations. Failing to plan for situations has dire results, inclusive of missed opportunities and expanded dangers.

Preparing for foreseen changes helps you neutralize boundaries and maximize possibilities. All your teams, including the finance and operations teams, can respond speedy without changing the business targets.

This method may be a prolonged strategic planning procedure for big organizations. Collecting and studying facts correctly can take months. Some of the elements that impact your strategic plans are drastic and might alternate speedy.

## 6. Blue Ocean approach

The Blue Ocean Strategy continuously pursues uncontested marketplace space via developing a completely unique and differentiated price proposition. A blue ocean refers to a extensive-open marketplace with a number of capability for increase and improvement. The opposite, purple oceans, is a market area with competition, and it could be hard to stand out.

Stop competing with different organizations and start carving out your own area of interest with the innovative Blue Ocean Strategy. With this strategic making plans model, you can extend your market proportion with the aid of targeting a previously untapped target audience.

The goal of this strategic making plans model isn't to outperform your competitors. It facilitates you redraw barriers within the industry and operate in a solo surroundings.

This strategic planning model proves customers do not need to pick between price and value - you can offer both. By figuring out what customers find valuable to your product or service, you may strategize the way to make it cheap without compromising first-rate.

Implementing the Blue Ocean Strategy facilitates you stable a aggressive aspect in an untapped market, appealing to new clients and growing your attain. You'll additionally find new avenues for increase and profitability – opening up larger, higher possibilities on your enterprise.

Some famous corporations that captured blue oceans are Netflix, iTunes, and Uber. All companies leveraged the Blue Ocean Strategy to create a unique value proposition that appealed to a broader target audience. They are currently some of the largest names available on the market.

By leveraging the Blue Ocean Strategy, you could keep away from the regular competition in red oceans and create uncontested market space.

**Want to attain a much wider target audience and raise your income?**

A strong strategic planning model could be the answer. With the right approach, you cannot best stay competitive, but outperform your opponents. You can also use this model alongside other planning techniques to supercharge your boom.

In this model, your organization have to explore a brand new subject without a sure foreseeable final results, making it surprisingly volatile. Finding the proper possibility calls for a whole lot of endurance and studies.

**SMART Validation Tool**

Most professionals use the SMART validation approach to make certain that goals (or Goals) in all methodologies are properly selected and drafted.

SMART Objectives are basically a primary guide and set of concrete rules for groups and business humans that need to use goals (or Goals) to resource in progressing their business. The SMART validation device makes a specialty of the constructing structure. It's represented by means of 5 key standards:

**Specific: What do you actually need to attain?**

Measurable: What stage of attempt, time, and cost will it take to attain that aim?

**Attainable:** Is the aim genuinely conceivable after weighing all of the execs and cons?

**Relevant:** Is the intention simply relevant to you and your business?

**Timely:** What are your cut-off dates, timelines, and measurable time restrictions?

**Aligning business goals with market demands and trends**

Trends are constantly moving within the business international, and staying in advance of the curve can provide you with a aggressive part. But how do you align your business with converting tendencies without dropping your center identification and price proposition? Here are a few strategies that will help you adapt and thrive in a dynamic environment.

## 1
### Scan the horizon

The first step to aligning your enterprise with changing tendencies is to pick out and reveal them. You can use various sources of information, inclusive of enterprise reports, client feedback, social media, competitor analysis, and market research, to identify rising patterns, needs, and possibilities. You have to also look past your instantaneous sector and remember the broader social, economic, technological, and environmental factors that may have an effect on your commercial enterprise inside the destiny.

## 2
### Evaluate the impact

Once you've got a clean picture of the traits which are relevant for your commercial enterprise, you want to assess how they'll have an effect on your cutting-edge and capability customers, your services and products, your procedures and operations, and your competitive role. You can use gear which includes SWOT evaluation, PESTEL analysis, state of affairs planning, and patron adventure mapping to evaluate the strengths, weaknesses, opportunities, and threats of every fashion, and the way they may impact your value proposition and commercial enterprise model.

## 3

**Adjust your strategy**

Based on your assessment, you can determine which traits to include, which to keep away from, and which to leverage for innovation. You can also need to adjust your imaginative and prescient, project, dreams, targets, and tactics to align your commercial enterprise with the converting trends. You can also need to expand new products and services, enter new markets, adopt new technology, or shape new partnerships. Whatever modifications you're making, you have to make sure that they're consistent together with your core values, brand identification, and client expectations.

## 4

**Communicate and have interaction**

Aligning your business with changing tendencies isn't always simplest a be counted of creating internal modifications, however also of speaking and attractive with your external stakeholders. You need to inform and teach your clients, employees, suppliers, buyers, and other relevant parties approximately the trends and the way they have an effect on your commercial enterprise. You have to also solicit their remarks, pointers, and thoughts, and involve them in the co-introduction of value. By communicating and tasty together with your stakeholders, you may build agree with, loyalty, and advocacy to your business.

## 5
**Experiment and examine**

Finally, aligning your enterprise with converting traits is an ongoing process that calls for constant experimentation and getting to know. You have to check your assumptions, measure your outcomes, and study from your successes and disasters. You must also screen the remarks loops and the feedback consequences of your moves at the traits and the market. You should be flexible and agile, and ready to pivot or iterate your approach as wished. By experimenting and gaining knowledge of, you can enhance your performance and stay in advance of the curve.

# Chapter 3: Leadership and Organizational Culture

In the complicated global of business, management plays a essential role in riding organizational success. The proper leadership can foster a tremendous paintings lifestyle, boost worker morale, and significantly enhance productiveness. Conversely, useless management can lead to disengagement, excessive turnover, and ultimately, an underperforming organization.

In this Guide, we are able to delve into the profound impact of leadership on organizational fulfillment and discover the approaches wherein effective leaders can drive their agencies in the direction of their desires.

Leadership and its Impact on Organizational Success

The concept of 'organizational success' transcends past mere economic profit. It's an amalgamation of several factors – employee satisfaction, client loyalty, marketplace reputation, and sustainable growth, to call some. In most of these aspects, leadership holds a pivotal position.

When we communicate about 'leadership effect', we talk over with the have an impact on exerted by way of leaders thru their choices, actions, and ordinary management style. This impact can appear in various methods – shaping the company's lifestyle, defining its imaginative and prescient and task, influencing worker behavior, and figuring out the organization's adaptability to alternate.

## The Power of Leadership in Shaping Organizational Culture

Organizational lifestyle is largely the character of a business enterprise. It encapsulates the business enterprise's values, ethics, expectations, and goals. Leaders play a essential function in defining and reinforcing this subculture. They set the tone for the agency, embody its values, and encourage employees to align their movements with the organization's ethos.

An organization with a strong, nice lifestyle is possibly to revel in higher worker engagement, lower turnover, and expanded productiveness. Moreover, organizations with a certainly described and nicely-communicated lifestyle frequently revel in superior brand popularity and client loyalty.

## Driving Employee Morale and Productivity through Leadership

One of the most major impacts of management is on worker morale and productivity. Effective leaders apprehend the significance of fostering a superb paintings environment in which employees experience valued, prompted, and engaged. They put money into their personnel' boom and development, offer optimistic feedback, and apprehend and reward their achievements.

When personnel sense encouraged and preferred, their productivity clearly will increase. They are more likely to move the more mile, contribute modern thoughts, and demonstrate loyalty to the employer. Hence, management plays a right away role in using worker productiveness, which in turn contributes to organizational achievement.

**Leadership and Strategic Direction**

Leaders are visionaries. They outline the strategic course of the company, setting clear goals, and formulating the strategies to attain them. A clean strategic course presents a roadmap for the agency, guiding decision-making at all tiers and making sure all efforts are aligned with the organization's desires.

By imparting a clean imaginative and prescient and direction, leaders can encourage their teams to paintings collaboratively towards shared dreams. This team spirit of purpose no longer most effective boosts performance and productivity however additionally contributes to a feel of belonging and dedication amongst employees.

**Leadership Impact on Change Management**

In today's unexpectedly evolving business landscape, change is inevitable. How an employer manages alternate can significantly affect its fulfillment? Leaders play a essential position in this procedure. They are liable for recognizing the need for trade, communicating it efficiently to their groups, and dealing with the transition while minimizing disruption.

Effective leaders are professional at main their agencies via change. They include exchange as an opportunity for boom, instilling this mindset in their teams. Their potential to manage change successfully can be a key determinant of an employer's resilience and adaptableness, contributing to its long-term success.

**The Bottom Line**

The impact of leadership on organizational achievement can't be overstated. Leaders are the using force at the back of an employer, steerage it in the direction of its dreams, shaping its culture, and influencing its typical overall performance. Their function in improving employee morale, presenting strategic course, and dealing with trade is crucial to the fulfillment of any organization.

Whether you're an aspiring chief or an established one, understanding the profound impact of your function is vital. By fostering a superb subculture, motivating your crew, providing clean strategic course, and navigating trade effectively, you may extensively contribute in your organization's success.

Remember, management is not approximately wielding authority; it's about inspiring others to obtain their high-quality. It's about setting the proper instance, promoting collaboration, and fostering an environment wherein innovation prospers. As a leader, your effect is some distance-accomplishing. Your actions and choices can form the future of your agency, and your management can be the catalyst that drives your organization toward its goals.

In the phrases of famed leadership professional John C. Maxwell, "A chief is one who knows the manner, goes the manner, and suggests the way." By know-how and embracing the effect of your leadership, you could guide your enterprise in the direction of unheard of achievement.

Lastly, let's not overlook that management, like some other skill, may be honed and stepped forward.

Continuous studying, self-mirrored image, and a genuine dedication on your function are the keys to turning into a powerful chief. Take benefit of leadership schooling applications, are trying to find feedback out of your group, and in no way forestall enhancing.

## How to Create a Continuous Improvement Culture?

In my profession, I actually have worked for organizations that embraced continuous improvement and those that did now not. The maximum successful ones already had an employee-centric agency subculture that allowed their people to feel secure enough to assignment the popularity quo and introduce new thoughts. In nowadays rapid-paced and aggressive commercial enterprise panorama, a lifestyle of non-stop development has to be embraced. Companies that actively promote a way of life of gaining knowledge of, innovation, and flexibility generally tend to outperform their counterparts.

A non-stop development culture is vital for the distribution enterprise to stay competitive, efficient and meet ever-converting consumer needs. Cultivating a lifestyle of continuous development can help facilitate the subsequent:

Improve efficiency: Finding methods to streamline procedures, reduce waste, optimize workflows, and leverage generation outcomes in faster throughput, lower fees, and the capability to scale operations.

Enhance high-quality: Continuous development specializes in reducing defects and errors via higher structures and schooling. This improves order accuracy, on-time transport, and patron pleasure.

Drive innovation: New thoughts and innovations emerge by way of empowering all employees to discover development opportunities. Companies can swiftly pilot and put into effect new technologies, strategies, and business models to advantage an edge.

Adapt to alternate: Customer expectations, demand patterns, and technologies constantly shift in distribution. A lifestyle of non-stop development positions agencies to unexpectedly adapt via ongoing training, comments loops, and iterative checking out of new processes.

Retain expertise: Employees need to work at agencies wherein their thoughts rely and they could develop new capabilities. The engagement round continuous improvement creates a collaborative and motivational way of life.

Boost competitiveness: Distribution is an more and more complex and competitive space. Companies that embed continuous development into their culture will outperform their peers in fee, nice, flexibility and innovation.

In addition, here are a handful of key attributes agencies, no matter enterprise or cognizance, can adopt to create a way of life of non-stop improvement.

Leadership's commitment to non-stop improvement: Establishing a tradition of continuous improvement begins on the top. While all innovation will no longer come from senior leaders, they have to reveal commitment to the system by using developing a secure surroundings to undertaking traditional information, placing clear expectancies, and allocating vital sources to innovation initiatives. When leaders prioritize and incentivize improvement tasks, employees apprehend the significance of non-stop improvement, which allows foster a increase and improvement mind-set all through the organization.

Encouraging open conversation and collaboration: Open and powerful communication fosters innovation and increase. Encourage personnel to voice their ideas, issues, and recommendations without worry of judgment or dismissal. While each idea won't be followed, a procedure of soliciting and reviewing them ought to. Establishing channels for comments and collaboration, which includes inspiration boxes, everyday team conferences, and innovation workshops, promotes a experience of possession and involvement. By embracing diverse perspectives and fostering go-purposeful collaboration, companies can tap into the collective intelligence in their workforce and drive meaningful change.

Embracing a mastering tradition: Organizations should foster a getting to know mind-set among employees.

Encourage ongoing expert development through education packages, workshops, conferences, and mentorship opportunities. By investing in employees' growth, groups empower individuals to collect new skills, live abreast of emerging tendencies, and make a contribution to the company's usual development efforts. Learning should be seen as a continuous journey rather than a one-time occasion, inspiring personnel to seek non-public and expert boom opportunities. These enterprise-funded possibilities are together useful.

**Focus on process improvement:**
Continuous improvement is not pretty much converting services or products. It is also approximately improving the underlying processes that support them. This approach figuring out and doing away with waste, decreasing errors, and improving efficiency. Regularly tune and speak development towards those goals, leveraging key overall performance indicators (KPIs) to degree success and identify areas for development.

**Data-pushed selection-making:**
Continuous development is based totally on facts, so organizations should gather and examine facts to

perceive regions for development. This records can assist music development, become aware of traits, and inform selections. Moving your agency useful resource planning (ERP) software and different systems to the cloud is step one in deploying new tools like artificial intelligence (AI) and machine learning (ML). Combining all of your information out of your disparate machine right into a single data lake allows you realize this ability.

During a latest communique with Jon Cox, chief deliver chain officer at Envoy Solutions, I asked, "Why is it important for an organization to have a tradition of non-stop improvement, and what does that appear like to you?" Jon spoke back, "Continuous improvement is vital to commercial enterprise sustainability. Variables are continuously changing round us, or as we love to remind ourselves, shifts occur. As a wholesale distributor, there are continually opportunities to enhance, that could include looking upstream to accomplice with the seller network, collaborating with customers downstream, or investing in technology to streamline procedures.

At Envoy Solutions, our continuous improvement mindset results in innovative answers that unlock fee for our stakeholders. I consider that when you empower your body of workers and interact them in the efforts to make upgrades; efficiency, productivity and innovation accelerates."

**The Final Word**

Creating a subculture of non-stop development is a journey that calls for commitment, collaboration, and a shared vision. It approach preserving a healthy level of dissatisfaction with properly outcomes and always striving to improve.

Whether you are the leader or an employee, you need to ask yourself a way to help your corporation stay ahead of the competition. Organizations can foster innovation, power sustainable boom, and enhance operational efficiency by implementing non-stop development strategies.

Employees will be empowered to develop professionally, make contributions their excellent ideas, and adapt to changing circumstances. As a end result, companies could be placed as leaders of their industries and be able to navigate the complexities of today's enterprise landscape.

## Building and nurturing high-performance teams

As a business proprietor or supervisor, you are likely aware of the importance of building high-performance teams. Working in a less-than-acceptable team environment can result in ongoing conflicts and a lack of motivation, whereas being a part of a a success, excessive-performing crew can be a rewarding and motivating revel in for every person involved.

This Guide explores the definition of excessive-performing teams and the characteristics you could look out for to identify one. We also discuss the only methods to build excessive-performance groups and broaden them inside your employer, and offer records on a number of the tools available to aid you with this.

**What is a excessive acting group?**

A high-acting crew is a group of folks who attempt for excellence thru -way open verbal exchange, mutual trust, common dreams, shared leadership, clear process roles, and constructive conflict. Each crew member accepts responsibility for his or her workload and moves.

**The benefits of high-performing teams consist of:**

A broad range of abilities and ability-sets
A organization of modern thinkers, each with their ideas and hints to carry to the desk
Little requirement for management enter
Improved morale
Better productivity
Characteristics of high acting groups
Individuals running inside excessive-acting teams can be described as being:

**Goal-oriented and formidable**

Committed to their colleagues and the general team task
Highly skilled

Experts in their subject

Collaborative, encouraging contribution from all crew individuals - together with the introverts

Innovative

Able to paintings to a excessive trendy

Willing to simply accept constructive criticism

Professor Ina Toe gel suggests that high-acting teams should be fashioned of no more than eight people - too many human beings approach "demanding situations in coordination, improved tension, and reduced productivity". She also advises thinking about using peer recruitment, enabling individuals of the present group to play a part inside the appeal and selection in their destiny friends.

Common styles of excessive performance team models
Structurally, excessive-performance teams are designed to enhance overall performance and attention at the information of delivering consequences. There are many distinctive variations that organizations use to establish their identification. Here are some examples:

**Work teams**

Work groups are liable for constant regions such as manufacturing, and customer support. They are a collection of employees whose specialties all lie within the same region. Whether it's miles generating goods or offering offerings, the paintings team is a generally strong, commonly complete-time, and well-described crew.

Found in both production and service companies, they are typically managed or directed by way of supervisors who make the wider choices in how it's miles accomplished and who does it. Self-dealing with teams concerning employees making choices that had been formerly made by supervisors are gaining want.

**Virtual teams**

Virtual teams allow agencies to curate groups of the pleasant expertise viable. Thanks to a global pandemic, we became very attuned to the opportunities, strengths, and weaknesses of a virtual crew. This is wherein a collection of people work together within the pursuit of common desires across time, area, and organizational obstacles.

Linked thru technology (i.e., Zoom, WebEx, internal networks), participants of a digital team coordinate their work predominantly with electronic verbal exchange tech to complete precise responsibilities and may never truly meet face-to-face. Because of the lack of geographical constrictions, groups are first-class located to obtain the quality skills viable to finish precise initiatives. They are equally regarded as greater efficient in costs of time and associated travel expenses.

**Project groups**

Project teams are transient groups which are assembled to finish particular tasks or responsibilities with a exact quit. They encompass individuals from one-of-a-kind departments who own specialized information and expertize required to achieve the preferred outcome.

One of the important thing benefits of task groups is that they convey together numerous perspectives and ability sets to tackle complicated demanding situations. They are not worried in repetitive tasks however alternatively focus on making use of them expertize and judgment to produce great results.

## Management groups

Management teams offer route to subordinate teams and oversee enterprise performance. The authority of a management group is derived from the hierarchical rank of its contributors, with executive control groups sitting at the pinnacle of the hierarchy.

These groups establish the strategic path of the business and manage overall performance through leveraging their collective expertize. They are accountable for making sure that the enterprise is jogging effectively and correctly.

## Parallel teams

Parallel teams are created whilst an company wishes to carry out features that its formal shape is not equipped to deal with. These teams commonly draw people from extraordinary paintings units or roles and function alongside the formal organizational structure.

Parallel teams have constrained decision-making authority however could make guidelines which could lead to wider changes inside the employer. They are often used to clear up issues and drive improvements, with examples which includes challenge forces, employee improvement agencies, and exceptional development teams.

## What are the roles in a high performance team?

High performance groups are critical to the fulfillment of any agency. Dr Raymond Meredith Belbin, a management theorist, identified nine one-of-a-kind roles which are essential for a team to feature correctly. Understanding these roles can assist crew members broaden their strengths and paintings collaboratively to manipulate weaknesses.

**Action Roles:**

Implementer: This person excels at translating the crew's ideas into practicable obligations and priorities.

Shaper (Task Leader): The Shaper is a dynamic position targeted on organizing goals and overcoming boundaries.

**Completer/Finisher:** This function is characterized by means of meticulousness, interest to detail, and the capacity to fulfill cut-off dates.

**People Skills Roles:**

Coordinator: The Coordinator is professional at facilitating decision-making and encouraging collaboration.

**Team Worker:** This man or woman is a good listener and excels at being cooperative, collaborative, and tactful.

**Resource Investigator:** The Resource Investigator is an extrovert who's skilled at making connections, collecting data, and exploring new opportunities.

**Cerebral/Intellectual Roles:**

**Plant:** This individual is skilled at hassle-fixing and wondering outdoor the box.

**Monitor/Evaluator:** The Monitor/Evaluator possesses suitable judgment and strategic thinking potential.

**Specialists:** Specialists provide technical oversight and expertize within their respective fields.

How to build and increase a high-performing group
Building a high-performing team is a vital part of any enterprise fulfillment. The characteristics of a high-appearing crew can vary depending at the company's targets, but one factor is certain - a excessive-performing group can assist pressure motivation, productivity and profitability.

These are seven key regions for managers to awareness on to build a high-appearing group.

## 1. Prioritize communique

Effective communique is one of the maximum essential characteristics of a high-acting group. By prioritizing communique, managers can ensure upgrades in motivation, productiveness and profitability.

To promote effective conversation, managers ought to encourage a robust recognition on team communique and prioritize the dissemination of data to their direct reviews. It is vital to assist group participants recognize their very own and others' preferred communication styles and to set up the exceptional method when it comes to group briefings or formal team conferences.

## 2. Set SMART targets

Setting clean objectives on the outset is one of the exceptional methods to make sure a excessive-acting group. Doing so will make certain the group knows exactly what they are running towards and how this contributes to the general fulfillment of the business.

Managers have to keep in mind setting up a goals assembly with the team as a discussion board to speak about key priorities. This lets in team members to have a few enter in the improvement of objectives, with any luck meaning they may be extra committed to accomplishing them.

## 3. Tackle battle

Even the quality high-appearing group within the global will still enjoy war once in a while. While in positive instances constrained struggle can be beneficial, the exceptional way to approach that is to count on it and be ready for it whilst it happens.

Then, as soon as an difficulty arises, set approximately addressing it as a depend of urgency. By resolving the warfare quick, managers can prevent it from spiraling out of control and causing a deeper rift.

## 4. Understand your cutting-edge and destiny dynamics

To flow a crew ahead, it is vital to recognize the dynamics of ways human beings are currently running. Managers should do not forget the subsequent questions:

Do you realize the strengths of the human beings running inside your crew?
Are you privy to any barriers which need to be improved upon?
What is the position of everybody in the team?
Why are they important?
How does the group react to trade?

Are there any drivers for ability conflict inside the group?

By running collaboratively with their groups to answer those questions, managers can identify any schooling wishes or ability gaps that can then be resolved to enhance future overall performance.

## 5. Master emotional intelligence

Emotional Intelligence (EI) is a powerful driver in relation to teamwork. When mastered effectively, it can assist transform understanding of the team's 'DNA'. EI may be defined as "the capacity to harmonize idea and emotion".

It calls for an man or woman to recognize and manage their own emotions while recognizing and handling those of different people. By always using the information given by way of EI, a team can communicate effectively and foster an attitude of loyalty and engagement. They can also be capable of best-music their crew running competencies to push for similarly fulfillment.

## 6. Establish trust

Trust is on the coronary heart of any a success crew. Without it, teams can be unable to progress because of worry of struggle or lack of commitment. Establishing accept as true with among crew individuals can help take the crew from best overall performance stages to wonderful effects.

Being open and honest approximately strengths and obstacles in administrative center behaviors is one way to assist generate consider between crew contributors. Having an expertise of our persona developments can assist us to study why we behave in a certain manner. It can also pick out how we interact with people and whether or not we want to recall making adjustments to our behavior.

**7. Feedback is a gift**
Remember to apprehend the work and achievement of the crew. Even if you are unable to offer monetary incentives, announcing 'thanks' often goes an extended manner in showing your staff that they're valued.

Benefits of constructing excessive performance groups for organizations
There are many advantages associated with constructing high performance teams, their effect can

be substantial with broader advantages to the enterprise, the contributors of the team and the personnel throughout the relaxation of the company as a whole.

The immediate reward for developing these groups for the enterprise is they meet the specific objective or triumph over the hassle the crew became created to work on. Whether that turned into to create a new consumer service product that addressed the wishes of the enterprise to increase a plan for a complicated office move or maybe create a brand new enterprise tradition designed to foster extra creativity or better time management practices.

A successful high performance group also can deliver lengthy-lasting overall performance benefits to the organization and its employees, even after the crew is disbanded or set to work on something else. A key to this is to create a focused, frictionless collaboration of the sort required to accomplish high-precedence objectives which can build believe amongst group participants whilst aligning the wider team of workers with the company's vision.

The blessings of building and constantly growing excessive overall performance teams inside the administrative center consist of the subsequent:

**Improved productiveness and efficiency**
One of the number one advantages of constructing high overall performance teams is improved productiveness and efficiency. High performing groups are made of specialists in their respective fields, who work collaboratively to obtain their desires. When team individual's paintings together, they could capitalize on their strengths and talents, ensuing in improved productiveness and efficiency.

**Challenging outcomes**
High performance groups are designed to attain tough consequences. These teams are strategically centered on the specific objective or trouble that wishes to be addressed. Whether it's far growing a brand new client provider product or developing a brand new corporation tradition, high performance team's paintings collaboratively to conquer complicated demanding situations.

Increased agree with and engagement with paintings

When group member's paintings collaboratively in the direction of reaching their dreams, it builds trust and engagement with their paintings. Team individuals learn to depend on every different and develop a feel of camaraderie, ensuing in elevated motivation and activity satisfaction.

## Business vision actualization

High overall performance groups help to actualize the enterprise vision. When teams work collaboratively to gain their shared objectives, it aligns the wider workforce with the corporation's imaginative and prescient. This ends in advanced performance and allows to gain outcomes for clients or internally that in addition the enterprise performance.

## Successful accomplishment of high-precedence goals

High overall performance groups are a hit in carrying out excessive-priority objectives. This is due to the focused, frictionless collaboration of crew contributors, who paintings collectively correctly to acquire their shared goals. As a result, corporations can reap their desires faster and with greater fulfillment.

## Maintaining excessive overall performance

Once high overall performance teams are formed, it's far critical to hold their overall performance. A written team constitution can help to provide readability on expectancies, and it is important to invite for contributions from the crew to empower them and make certain they're on board with the desires from the beginning.

Businesses should additionally be transparent about their efforts and get the whole crew on board by making a collective commitment to individual and team improvements. Regularly updating and dispensing the business case for excessive performance groups also can help to make sure that everybody is aligned with the imaginative and prescient and desires.

# Chapter 4: Operational Excellence

Operational performance indicates the fulfillment of an corporation's execution of its middle commercial enterprise strategy. The prosperity of an enterprise is fundamentally anchored in its operational overall performance. By improving operational overall performance, corporations can improve productiveness, lessen expenses, and improve consumer pride. This enhancement is focused around enhancing several operational elements, including method performance, useful resource utilization, and inter-departmental coordination.

Two crucial factors that contribute to a flourishing enterprise are marketing and operations. Marketing consists of the advertising of products or services and attracting customers, while operations make sure the well timed, value-powerful, and specification-compliant achievement of purchaser orders. As a enterprise expands, especially for the duration of intervals of speedy growth, the significance of operations turns into increasingly paramount.

It's now not unusual for leaders of small businesses to overlook the significance of operations in scaling their groups. Some even display disinterest in operations, opting as an alternative to recognition on strategic imaginative and prescient. This lack of knowledge and hobby often leads to operational failures, which could have dramatic and seen results for a enterprise. Despite its invisibility, operational achievement is important for sustainable increase and consumer pleasure. Therefore, it is crucial to strike a balance among marketing and operations for long-term profitability and sustainability.

Behind the scenes, operational teams work tirelessly to make sure consumer orders are fulfilled on time, inside finances, and within specification. Revenue operations (RevOps) inspire transparency and collaboration among advertising and marketing and operations groups to reap consumer pleasure and profitability. While Lean and Six Sigma frameworks can seem intimidating for small organizations, efforts are being made to make this statistic available to them. The RevOps movement goals to dismantle silos among advertising and operations and consciousness on client delight and profitability. Balancing advertising and operations is essential for sustainable achievement in business.

For example, manufacturing groups like Freudenberg NOK Sealing Technologies and Belden Inc. have correctly carried out non-stop improvement applications. Freudenberg NOK Sealing Technologies has been implementing its "growth" lean application for 25 years, completing over ninety-four,000 lean and six sigma projects and saving $414 million. The key to a a hit software is making sure it is important to the company and its management. Continuous development applications need to adapt and adapt through the years, with ordinary tests and refinements to maintain them fresh. Learning and sharing nice practices is important for non-stop development, with applications like dependent fine exercise change days assisting to unfold successful techniques throughout the enterprise.

Training and empowering personnel is critical for keeping a culture of non-stop improvement.

Belden Inc. holds an annual lean international cup opposition to understand breakthrough approaches done the usage of lean methodologies. The competition brings teams from throughout the business enterprise together to share studies and study from every different. The lean world cup opposition is a giant funding in terms of money and time however offers treasured advantages in terms of sharing fine practices and improving internal procedures.

Freudenberg NOK Sealing Technologies has finished over 94,000 lean and six sigma tasks inside the beyond 25 years, ensuing in savings of $414 million. Freudenberg NOK Sealing Technologies has educated over a hundred thirty licensed lean system and six sigma black belts. Belden Inc has 10 years of lean enjoy and holds an annual Lean World Cup opposition. The triumphing crew of the Lean World Cup in 2017 carried out a comprehensive cost circulation transformation and accomplished great improvements in setup time reduction and assembly area efficiency. The Lean World

Cup opposition brings collectively teams from distinct functions globally to percentage reports and enhance internal tactics. The Lean World Cup opposition involves full-size investment in phrases of time and money, but the blessings outweigh the fees.

"There are only 3 guidelines you can go in commercial enterprise: you may cross backward and lose momentum, you may live the direction and hope it really is sufficient, or you could enhance, get better at what you do, and grasp new possibilities." - Matthew Portu, President of Freudenberg NOK Sealing Technologies. "You cannot hold a culture alive unless your education your human beings and also you empower them to use it." - Vicky Jandreau, Director of Growth in North America at Freudenberg NOK Sealing Technologies. "It is identified as a massive accomplishment inner Belden." - Jerry Rose, Vice President of Lean Enterprise at Belden Inc.

Freudenberg NOK has applied their "growth" program for 25 years, which specializes in lean implementation and removing waste thru group concord. They have completed over 94,000 lean and six sigma initiatives, resulting in financial savings of $414 million. The software stays on the heart of their organizational tradition and has enabled them to cognizance on non-stop development.

Belden Inc., a worldwide manufacturer of connectivity and networking products, has been training lean manufacturing for a decade. They maintain an annual "Lean World Cup" competition, wherein groups from throughout the organization publish breakthrough methods achieved the usage of lean methodologies. The competition recognizes and celebrates the accomplishments of those groups and promotes engagement in executing tremendous improvements. The competition is not confined to manufacturing operations and consists of teams from finance and customer support as properly.

Both Freudenberg NOK and Belden emphasize the significance of continuous gaining knowledge of in their lean applications. Freudenberg NOK has carried out structured satisfactory exercise exchange days, where attendees visit production websites that display main best practices. This permits for the sharing of information and the implementation of successful practices in different centers. Belden also emphasizes studying thru their Lean World Cup opposition, in which team's percentage their experiences and stories around their lean sports. These studying opportunities help to improve internal processes and drive continuous development.

## 2. Streamlining Processes for Enhanced Efficiency

Enhancing operational performance revolves around the meticulous refinement of techniques, a journey that includes figuring out and casting off needless steps inside the elaborate net of methods to reduce complexity. The remaining purpose is to establish a streamlined workflow that minimizes waste and propels productivity to new heights. This objective may be performed by means of several means, such as process mapping, lean manufacturing techniques, and continuous development projects.

Streamlined tactics are not simply about simplifying processes however optimizing them as well. Tools consisting of crucial databases play a crucial position right here. These systems consolidate all relevant facts, which includes gadget records, maintenance schedules, and work orders, facilitating easier access and retrieval of statistics, extensively reducing facts search time, and enhancing normal performance.

Predictive protection techniques, along with condition tracking and real-time data evaluation, also come into play. These techniques continuously monitor the circumstance of system and belongings, permitting the identity of potential issues earlier than they amplify into primary troubles. This proactive maintenance approach minimizes downtime, further optimizing operational efficiency.

Automation is any other vital aspect of manner streamlining. Routine duties consisting of information entry or document generation may be automated, decreasing manual attempt and increasing manner performance. Automated workflows for protection approaches additionally contribute to stepped forward productiveness.

Integrating unique structures and technologies can beautify the streamlining procedure. For instance, integrating preservation control software program with employer aid making plans (ERP) structures like Oracle Fusion Cloud and SAP Extended Warehouse Management can permit seamless information sharing, improving typical visibility and manipulate.

The process of streamlining is a continuous cycle of figuring out bottlenecks and regions of development, making sure consistency and duty. This may be done through comprehensive documentation, the usage of templates, and the implementation of computerized renovation control structures (CMMS).

In the context of startups, the importance of speed and agility is paramount. Startups often face the mission of moving slowly, a scenario that may be rectified by avoiding the confusion of activity with development. True progress is described via the speed at which a product is released, achieves product-marketplace match, and grows. This necessitates prioritization, allowing startups to focus on what's maximum important and resist the temptation to do the entirety without delay.

Creating minimum possible procedures can save you useless delays and inefficiencies, allowing startups to transport quicker. Regular assessment of ordinary strategies is crucial to make certain they scale with growth. Hiring the proper human beings for the right roles is likewise an crucial part of a startup's fulfillment, permitting CEOs to delegate and scale operations. In the stop, prioritization, manner development, and hiring well can help startups build a a success enterprise quicker.

## 3. Leveraging Technology to Automate Processes

The plain has an effect on of generation in boosting operational abilities is no longer a point of debate. Incorporating automation technology along with Robotic Process Automation (RPA) and Artificial Intelligence (AI) transforms repetitive, mundane responsibilities into computerized tactics. This shift now not only permits your team to cognizance on strategic duties that upload cost but additionally elevates usual performance.

Consider the Indie Hackers community, a thriving community of marketers and creatives. It has leveraged automation to shop countless hours for impartial software businesses, permitting them to deal with important duties. Tools like Zippier and Integrate were successfully employed to automate obligations starting from statistics access to customer service, resulting in a extraordinary four hundred hours stored in keeping with month, mitigating the want for additional hires and fostering scalability.

Furthermore, predictive analytics and system studying technologies have the capacity to revolutionize selection-making techniques. By predicting destiny tendencies, those tools enable groups to make information-driven selections, thereby enhancing operational performance.

The price of automation is likewise obvious in task automation. Implementing automation software simplifies and accelerates workflows, decreasing the want for guide hard work. Task automation has been confirmed to keep as much as 30% of time spent on repetitive tasks, paving the way for improved productiveness and enterprise increase.

Several actual-international examples of a hit assignment automation exist. Dell Technologies, as an instance, employed Robotic Process Automation (RPA) to automate high-extent HR strategies, growing productiveness by means of a marvelous eighty-five%. Similarly, the British Museum used the social media automation device Hoot suite to growth their social media engagement via 126%.

By incorporating automation technology and predictive analytics into their operations, corporations can have unfastened their crew to concentrate on higher-fee tasks, are expecting destiny traits, and make facts-pushed decisions. This leads to a large enhancement of operational overall performance.

When enforcing robotic procedure automation in business maintenance structures, start via figuring out the repetitive obligations that can be automated. This should encompass producing paintings orders, scheduling upkeep sports, or engaging in recurring inspections. Once recognized, software robots or bots can be evolved to perform these activities autonomously, decreasing the need for manual intervention.

Artificial intelligence (AI) packages can enhance efficiency and selection-making processes in asset management structures. AI algorithms can analyze large amounts of records and pick out patterns and developments which might be difficult for humans to figure. This can help asset management structures optimize portfolio performance, pick out ability dangers, and make informed investment choices.

Predictive analytics can offer several advantages in business operations. It can help optimize maintenance schedules by using predicting when equipment or machinery is likely to fail. This permits for proactive upkeep, reducing downtime and improving typical operational efficiency.

Various machine studying techniques may be used to optimize preservation tactics. These strategies can assist expect device failures, identify most suitable preservation schedules, and optimize resource allocation.

When integrating AI into commercial protection structures, there are several high-quality practices to remember. First, it's miles critical to acquire and analyze relevant facts from the maintenance systems to pick out styles and capacity areas for improvement. This records can encompass historic protection records, system performance information, and sensor readings.

Robotic Process Automation (RPA) and Artificial Intelligence (AI) can offer numerous benefits in improving operational efficiency. RPA can automate repetitive and rule-based obligations, decreasing mistakes and increasing productiveness. AI can examine huge amounts of information and offer insights and predictions, permitting organizations to make records-driven choices and optimize techniques. Together, RPA and AI can streamline workflows, enhance accuracy, and loose up human employees to recognition on greater complicated and cost-delivered tasks. This can result in cost financial savings, faster processing times, advanced client experiences, and typical operational efficiency.

## 4. Making Data More Accessible: The Role of Integration Platforms

Integration answers like Makini are key gamers in enhancing operational overall performance by using making statistics greater accessible. These platforms merge business upkeep and asset control structures, supplying a complete view of statistics. The need to navigate multiple structures is removed, saving time and ensuring that decision makers have access to accurate, real-time facts.

Consider the case of Geisinger Health Plan (GHP), which exemplifies how integration can improve operational performance. GHP leveraged the combination of Kyruus and HealthSparq to decorate its digital issuer directory. This integration enabled get right of entry to to richer, extra correct information immediately sourced from health structures in the Kyruus network. This ended in good sized enhancements in the profiles of participating carriers inside the GHP listing, enabling members to make extra informed healthcare choices. The result turned into a fifty-four% growth in general profile interactions.

Another example is Pfizer's partnership with Fig share. Pfizer created the Pfizer Fig share portal to host simple language summaries and supplemental statistics associated with posted manuscripts. The portal helps numerous report sorts and lets in for content download, which has increased the visibility and impact of Pfizer's studies. The portal has been specifically beneficial for sharing supplemental substances such as research facts, tables, pictures, motion pictures, and software program. The achievement of this initiative is obvious from the portal's usage metrics, with content being considered over 1,000 instances and downloaded 200 times.

The reports of GHP and Pfizer underscore the transformative ability of integration platforms. By ensuring seamless get entry to accurate, up to date facts, those systems can significantly beautify operational overall performance and selection-making.

Makini stands out as one such platform, presenting a variety of integrations for exclusive industrial operations. It lets in users to combine one of a kind structures and technologies, enabling seamless information change and improved performance in commercial procedures. By the use of Makini for records integration, commercial operations can gain from streamlined workflows, real-time records synchronization, and better visibility into operations. This can cause better decision-making, decreased manual efforts, and expanded productivity.

Several first-rate practices can be applied to improve operational performance with Makini. Proper integration with other structures, together with Oracle Fusion Cloud Warehouse Management, is vital for seamless facts sharing and streamlined operational processes. Leveraging Makini's use cases can offer insights into a way to optimize operations for better overall performance. Regularly reviewing and analyzing the facts generated by using Makini can help pick out areas of improvement and tell choices to enhance operational efficiency. Continuous training and schooling of employees on a way to efficiently use Makini is also essential.

For example, Makini has been used to seamlessly integrate facts from distinctive assets to enhance general commercial enterprise strategies and choice-making abilties. Companies have correctly streamlined their upkeep approaches with Makini, resulting in progressed productiveness and decreased downtime.

Choosing the right integration platform for industrial preservation and asset control structures requires thinking about numerous factors. Compatibility with current structures and technologies, scalability and flexibility, safety capabilities, ease of use, and the popularity and tune report of the platform company are all crucial concerns. Makini checks a lot of these packing containers, imparting integrations with numerous systems, such as Oracle Fusion Cloud Warehouse Management and Inform WMS.

Setting up records integration with Makini involves following step-via-step instructions available at the Makini website. The setup process is simple, and aid is available if any issues are encountered.

In sum, Makini is a platform that gives facts integration services for business operations. It gives capabilities and abilities to facilitate seamless statistics integration in industrial settings. The platform supports integration with diverse structures, which includes Oracle Fusion Cloud Warehouse Management and SAP Extended Warehouse Management. By leveraging Makini, commercial operations can beautify their facts integration techniques and improve typical performance

## 5. Optimizing Resources for Better Operational Performance

Managing resources effectively is a cornerstone of improving operational overall performance. This assignment encompasses strategic aid usage, whether or not it involves human sources, equipment, or substances, to enhance efficiency and productivity. Key techniques such as ability planning, stock manage, and body of workers scheduling are pivotal in improving aid utilization.

Capacity planning in commercial renovation employs diverse techniques to make sure efficient resource use and most reliable performance. These encompass ancient facts analysis, predictive preservation, staff management, system utilization tracking, and era adoption. Historical statistics on device utilization, protection schedules, and downtime can provide insights into potential requirements. Predictive protection, powered by means of advanced analytics and gadget gaining knowledge of algorithms, can forecast equipment failures and upkeep desires. Efficient personnel management ensures the availability of skilled technicians and schedules renovation sports primarily based on aid availability. Monitoring gadget utilization metrics together with uptime, downtime, and cycle time can offer treasured insights for potential planning. Lastly, adopting virtual equipment and technologies like automated preservation management systems (CMMS) and IOT sensors can notably enhance ability planning.

Inventory manage in asset control structures can be optimized by way of imposing a centralized gadget for tracking and handling inventory, conducting everyday audits, establishing efficient workflows and tactics, and utilizing barcode or RFID generation for easy identification and tracking of assets. Proactive call for forecasting and replenishment can in addition assist optimize inventory stages and minimize stock outs or extra stock.

Workforce scheduling in industrial protection helps optimize the group of workers by way of making sure the proper technicians are assigned to the proper tasks on the proper time. This approach can lead to expanded productivity and efficiency in upkeep operations, lessen downtime, and provide visibility into technician availability and workload, taking into consideration powerful useful resource allocation.

Predictive upkeep is a proactive method that is vital in stopping gadget screw ups and lowering downtime. This strategy not best guarantees top-rated equipment use however additionally extends its lifespan, decreasing the need for frequent replacements or maintenance. By reading real-time statistics from the system to discover ability problems or anomalies, predictive analytics and machine studying algorithms can perceive styles and traits that suggest the likelihood of device failure. This permits proactive scheduling of protection activities and addressing capability problems before they result in breakdowns.

However, resource optimization must be approached with a nuanced angle. As outlined inside the e-book "This is Lean," an immoderate awareness on resource performance can inadvertently result in an boom in workload, thereby rendering the organization much less green. Therefore, it is important to balance aid performance with basic operational performance. Companies which have successfully implemented this balanced method have pronounced great upgrades in their operational performance. Thus, while aid optimization is absolutely crucial, it have to now not be pursued at the rate of average operational efficiency.

## 6. Enhancing Cross-Team Collaboration in Industrial Operations

The significance of go-useful collaboration in enhancing operational overall performance is crucial. When people from diverse departments inside an employer work collectively toward not unusual objectives, the outcome is stepped forward problem-fixing, quicker decision-making, and green purpose attainment.

Establishing clear commonplace objectives, common interplay, and team-constructing sports are key to fostering this collaboration. The use of collaborative tools and technology can function a catalyst in this technique, permitting teams to paintings collectively correctly, regardless of their area or time zone.

However, reaching effective cross-purposeful collaboration can be hard because of problems along with bad conversation, lack of duty, and conflicting priorities. To conquer these demanding situations, it's important to improve communique great, discover professionals inside teams, and interact in cross-useful crew building.

Creating a subculture that promotes information sharing and ordinary group conferences can be transformative. It fosters innovation, boosts worker engagement, and enhances conversation abilities, thereby enriching the organizational way of life. Moreover, a place of work environment that nurtures mutual appreciate and believe can appreciably enhance collaboration.

In the context of software program engineering for medium-sized distributed medical projects, the Institute for the Design of Advanced Energy Systems (IDAES) exemplifies successful pass-functional collaboration. They carried out 3 beneficial strategies: weekly complete team developer conferences, incremental automation, and "soapboxing" software engineering in reputable dreams and deliverables.

Weekly meetings permit for go-slicing problem resolution, practice dissemination, and camaraderie building. The incremental automation strategy regularly carries automated testing practices to beautify group productivity. "Soapboxing" includes emphasizing key factors of software engineering and improvement practices to attract the eye of undertaking management and funders.

The ultimate aim is to reduce friction inside the software program engineering surroundings and cultivate a experience of unity within the group. This now not handiest improves operational performance however additionally fosters collaboration, putting the level for organizational success.

Cross-team collaboration in operational overall performance affords several benefits. By uniting individuals from different teams and departments, agencies can foster a lifestyle of shared gaining knowledge of and understanding alternate. This collaboration can lead to improved trouble-fixing abilities as group contributors carry numerous perspectives and knowledge to the table.

Furthermore, cross-team collaboration can enhance verbal exchange and coordination, ensuing in extra green and streamlined operational tactics. It can also sell innovation and creativity as distinctive teams work collectively to generate new thoughts and answers.

With clear conversation channels and ordinary conversation between groups, corporations can decorate go-group collaboration and ultimately improve normal crew overall performance and productivity. The introduction of opportunities for move-group collaboration, consisting of organizing cross-useful projects or assigning team individuals to paintings on different teams temporarily, can help foster relationships and enhance collaboration between teams.

Moreover, offering education and improvement opportunities to team contributors can also enhance move-group collaboration. This can encompass workshops or seminars on effective communique, group-building activities, and management improvement packages.

Overall, cross-crew collaboration in operational performance can contribute to progressed productiveness, effectiveness, and overall performance of a business enterprise.

## 7. Regular Reviews: The Key to Continuous Process Improvement

Enhancing operational performance is an ongoing adventure, and significant to this adventure is the steady refinement of techniques. This refinement comes from a scientific approach of everyday evaluations aimed at preserving most suitable performance requirements. These evaluations are not just a take a look at inside the container but a proactive technique to unearth capability areas of development.

Regular evaluation meetings, attended by using the organization's leaders, stakeholders, and other key employees worried in the operations, form the backbone of this systematic method. The structure of these conferences helps a complete knowledge of the method, its strengths, and its capacity regions for improvement.

Three important questions manual those evaluate meetings: in which must we focus, why did this show up, and who will do what via when. This technique ensures that the evaluate process has a clear route and the discussions are targeted, purposeful, and result-oriented. It is through those meetings that the overall performance of the operations is classified, and the important thing dreams are evaluated.

The objective of those conferences is to decorate operational performance, and to attain this, it is crucial to consciousness on a pick set of troubles. The leader of the review assembly performs a vital position in directing the point of interest in the direction of those issues and making sure that the dialogue remains on the right track. The cognizance must be on know-how the foundation causes of both precise and horrific effects, the usage of strategies like the five whys. This helps in identifying the real issues that want to be addressed for the development of operations.

The evaluate process is not pretty much identifying the issues but additionally approximately locating answers and movements to cope with those troubles. The overview conferences have to finish with the identification of unique moves that want to be taken for the improvement of operations. These moves are then assigned to the applicable employees, who're accountable for their implementation.

The leaders of the evaluation meetings ought to prepare for those meetings with the aid of studying the information and figuring out the key areas for development. This lets in for a greater targeted and effective dialogue all through the assembly. It is also important to keep away from stepping into the minutiae and focus on the substance of the troubles all through these meetings.

In huge agencies, it might be necessary to have cascading reviews, in which specific ranges of the organization talk exceptional metrics and problems. This ensures that everyone elements of the operations are protected inside the assessment manner. To keep music of the movements diagnosed in the course of those critiques, it's far crucial to have reliable systems in area.

Continuous technique improvement is a cornerstone for boosting operational overall performance. Regular reviews provide an opportunity to assess the cutting-edge country of operations, identify areas for development, and take necessary actions to improve performance. It is through this systematic and dependent approach that companies can obtain their strategic dreams and objectives.

## 8. Reducing Costs and Boosting Profits via Improved Operational Performance

Optimizing operational overall performance can lead to sizeable cost discounts and income increases. By improving efficiency, automating obligations, optimizing resources, and fostering collaboration, businesses can lower waste, raise productiveness, and heighten client pride. These improvements can translate into decrease operating costs, higher revenues, and in the end, augmented earnings.

Optimize your operational overall performance and increase your profits nowadays!

Strategies to beef up operational performance are consequently worthy investments.

Consider the Hubble Space Telescope (HST) task, undertaken by way of the US Air Force Center for Systems Engineering. Despite several structures engineering demanding situations, the venture executed fulfillment by way of using a balanced mixture of humility and optimism. One unique take a look at fixture specification error cost $10 million to rectify, illustrating the escalating price of defect correction in successive life cycle levels. Notwithstanding such limitations, the HST keeps to orbit Earth, accumulating astronomical statistics in the close to-infrared and ultraviolet spectra. The HST's fulfillment underscores the significance of stakeholder involvement, early participation in application definition, systems integration, life cycle guide planning, and hazard control.

John Deere's international organization offers another enlightening instance. The group initiated an agile transformation aimed toward improving speed and outcomes. Senior leadership determined to launch a complete transformation that could permeate each issue of the institution's paintings, together with application improvement, core infrastructure, and client-facing products. The Scrum and Scrum Scale frameworks were selected for their scalability across the commercial enterprise, and the implementation of the Agile Operating Model (AOM) included schooling, coaching, and help from Scrum Inc. The final results of this change passed preliminary goals, main to extended output, reduced time to market, improved engineering ratio, and cost performance. The agile transformation fostered a tradition that values continuous development and innovation.

Transform your organization with an agile technique and unencumber new stages of efficiency and innovation!

These case research serve as compelling proof to the profound impact that enhancing operational performance may have on an organization's bottom line. By streamlining tactics, automating responsibilities, optimizing sources, and improving collaboration, organizations can lessen waste, increase productiveness, and improve patron pride.

To streamline procedures and enhance operational overall performance, agencies can do not forget implementing various strategies. These include automation technology which includes robot method automation (RPA) or synthetic intelligence (AI), standardization of techniques and workflows across special departments or capabilities, adoption of lean concepts, generation integration consisting of company resource planning (ERP) and client courting management (CRM) systems, worker training and development applications, overall performance size tools and metrics, and fostering collaboration and powerful communique amongst teams.

In addition to those strategies, businesses can remember the use of integrations provided by way of Makini.Io to automate obligations and beautify operational efficiency. These integrations, together with Oracle Fusion Cloud Warehouse Management and SAP Extended Warehouse Management, can streamline and automate diverse operational duties, lowering manual attempt and enhancing basic performance.

Moreover, by means of using stock optimization answers supplied through Makini.Io, agencies can higher manage their inventory tiers and reduce wearing expenses. These solutions leverage facts analytics and forecasting algorithms to identify most advantageous inventory levels, limit stock outs, and ensure efficient replenishment.

Collaboration equipment also can be utilized to enhance teamwork and operational overall performance. This equipment can assist team members speak, share documents, and work together more successfully.

To lessen waste and boom efficiency, groups can don't forget imposing a Warehouse Management System (WMS) like the one presented by using Makini. This can automate tasks together with stock control, order success, and logistics, thereby minimizing mistakes and decreasing waste.

Finally, via imposing green methods, optimizing useful resource allocation, and enhancing service quality, groups can enhance customer pride. Regular tracking of key overall performance signs (KPIs) can assist become aware of areas for improvement and measure the effect of operational changes on purchaser delight.

Improve customer delight and pressure growth via monitoring your KPIs and making information-pushed operational improvements!

## Implementing lean and agile practices

Waste is highly-priced! ❧ It's paying a person no longer do any real paintings, deciding to buy supplies you don't want, or paying for team participants to kind out a preventable problem. Lean agile pursuits to do away with wasteful assets and tasks for advanced efficiency and reduced charges — whilst by no means sacrificing first-rate. In reality, lean agile prioritizes bringing cost to the customer with each choice that's made.

Lean agile is an improvement method that helps groups pick out waste and refine approaches. It's a guiding mindset that facilitates efficiency, effectiveness, and continuous improvement.

Consider this: You probably paintings lots better whilst your table isn't completely blanketed with a mess of things you don't need. When you eliminate distractions and waste, it establishes an organized workspace and workflow. This enables you focus on what's maximum crucial, making sure you work efficiently and effectively.

Here, you'll research greater about the improvement of lean, the advantages of lean agile, and the 5 core standards of lean.

## The development of lean agile

Lean agile, or lean software program improvement, originates from the ideas of lean manufacturing. The idea turned into delivered into production to improve earnings with the aid of lowering charges instead of entirely counting on accelerated income. If a corporation can eliminate waste and grow to be more efficient, it could shop money, thereby increasing normal income.

Lean agile is an agile method that, in basic terms, is pretty simple: improve performance with the aid of eliminating waste. Unlike conventional, waterfall undertaking control, which dictates a fixed plan laid out by means of a undertaking supervisor, lean agile strives to reduce all obligations and activities that don't provide real price. This helps ensure all and sundry concerned in a mission or product development can paintings at top-quality efficiency.

If you're looking to dive into the records of lean agile, Lean Enterprise Institute Inc., based in 1997 through James P. Womack, PhD, is a main useful resource for lean method. It targets to help humans and groups paintings higher through lean thinking and practices.

Lean practices are famous due to the fact they can be applied to different agile tactics and software improvement techniques. Lean agile provides a clear application for scaling agile, which is often tough for large or developing groups.

**The blessings of lean agile**

In case you're no longer on board with lean agile yet, allows evaluation its principal benefits.

**Waste much less time**

Time is wasted whilst processes don't run smoothly. In lean production, it's important for goods and offerings to be brought quickly and efficiently. No one's time should be wasted at the process, and agencies must intention for shorter lead instances without sacrificing first-class.

Wasting time in any industry is pricey, however it's mainly essential to pay attention whilst working in agile software development. Even a small bottleneck or broken process can absolutely throw off a workflow or product deadline. Lean agile enables improvement groups manipulate time successfully to make certain everybody is applied, nobody's time is wasted, and roadblocks are predicted earlier.

**Reduce fees**

When organizations eliminate waste, they store cash. In its original form, lean manufacturing ensured companies had the right amount of substances, personnel, and operating hours at any given time. Overproduction, over hiring, or certainly having too many substances to save are high priced wastes that can be eliminated via better control of systems and tactics.

Any business, irrespective of the enterprise, will shop money with advanced performance. Lean agile ensures that waste is constantly eliminated and agile groups hold to high-quality-track tactics for superior efficiency.

**Improve work great**

With lean agile, it's now not best approximately efficiency — it's approximately preserving efficient tactics even as bringing a quality product to customers and stakeholders. When organizations deliberately improve procedures, they stay competitive. Lean concepts recollect the purchaser value of any movement or selection to ensure wishes are usually met or handed.

**The 5 concepts of lean agile**

There are five center ideas for implementing lean technique:

Value

Value circulation

Flow

Pull

Perfection

These concepts describe a five-step procedure that guides the implementation of lean techniques for production, software program development teams, and other agile working towards industries.

**1. Identify price**

The first step requires you to step into the shoes of the consumer. Value is what the client needs and wants from a selected project or product.

Consider from the customers' point of view: What are their expectancies? What are they inclined to pay for? How do they want their wishes met?

Sometimes, clients may be not able to outline exactly what they're looking for — especially if it's a new product or generation they're unfamiliar with.

In any case, the task cannot circulate ahead without in reality figuring out what it will take to provide customer pride. You'll need to discover the cease aim (price) customers are hoping to find with the product or service.

**2. Map the price circulate**
Next, the team visually maps each of the stairs and strategies it will take to deliver the product from inception to transport. By making every step seen and always retaining the fee pinnacle-of-mind, it's easier to look which steps don't at once make a contribution to

continuous shipping. Once wasteful steps are discovered, the team finds approaches to do away with those steps or reduce them as a whole lot as feasible.

Getting rid of waste guarantees your agency doesn't unnecessarily invest in steps and approaches that don't upload cost. And — most significantly — the consumer gets precisely what they're seeking out.

### 3. Create drift

Once the waste is removed from the price flow, the subsequent step is making sure the final techniques paintings as efficiently and successfully as feasible, this means that no delays, disruptions, or bottlenecks. It's critical for the stairs that create cost to paintings in tight sequences to make certain the product flows smoothly in the direction of the purchaser.

In order to obtain this type of agile transformation, lean companies have to educate their employees to be adaptive and multi-professional, create cross-purposeful teams, smash down and reconfigure steps within the production, and balance employee workloads.

**4. Establish a pull gadget**

With more advantageous flow, your crew can deliver services and products quicker. A pull device allows "simply-in-time" production and delivery, limiting stock and work in development (WIP) gadgets by simplest generating sufficient to meet customer demand.

By setting up a pull system, you create services and products as needed as opposed to creating them earlier, which results in a growing stock or listing of duties that need to be saved and managed — draining your bottom line.

**5. Seek perfection**

By completing steps 1-four, waste is removed — for now. However, the paintings is by no means finished. There is constantly a technique that might be advanced, and there will usually be steps in challenge and product development that waste time and money or don't deliver fee. That's why the 5th step of searching for perfection is prime.

Lean takes time to put into effect, and going thru the system as soon as isn't sufficient. Build a non-stop improvement mindset into your enterprise lifestyle, and in no way settle for the equal antique.

## Quality management and performance metrics

SELECTING PERFORMANCE MEASURES & METRICS

Quality Glossary Definition: Performance standards

Also referred to as: choice metrics

Performance metrics are defined as statistics and challenge-unique information used to represent and verify an employer's great, abilities, and abilities. Performance metrics are defined differently in each enterprise and might change based on a organization's products and services. Common overall performance metrics encompass income, return on funding, consumer pride, industry and client evaluations, and a employer's reputation with its clients.

One of the biggest troubles associated with non-stop improvement and trouble fixing is the choice of the most suitable performance measures or fine performance metrics.

## ORGANIZATIONAL AND ENTERPRISE-LEVEL PERFORMANCE MEASURES

The world of trade and enterprise uses quite a few economic performance measures or overall performance metrics on the organizational and company degree. These encompass ratios including go back on funding (ROI) and return on net belongings (RONA).

These ratios and different non-economic ratios including market share and call recognition index, are structured variables that numerically describe the extent of achievement or failure of an company for a particular period of time, including one sector of a monetary yr.

However, the approaches wherein companies gain those levels of fulfillment or failure is of more significance (see Figure 1 under). Independent variables, inclusive of client pride indices, illness fees, and provider functionality indices, offer this statistic. When those factors mirror properly on a company, their based variables are more likely to reflect overall agency fulfillment.

These metrics may be handled as established variables with an entirely new set of unbiased variables along with conveyor speeds, temperature settings, spindle speeds, and paintings-in-system (WIP) ranges. The unbiased variables are direct measures of the strategies that make up the corporation structures growing products and services that generate organizational earnings.

When figuring out what performance measures or performance metrics to use for a machine, manner, or step within a technique, it can be beneficial to first determine what's important to customers (both inner or outside) and may be measured or counted.

If this cannot be responded immediately, recall what's critical to the patron that cannot be immediately measured or counted but can be assessed circuitously, the usage of one or greater proxy measures.

A sequence of top-down performance measures or performance metrics can show this method to non-stop improvement.

| Independent Variables | Dependent Variables |
|---|---|
| Customer satisfaction | Market share |
| On-time delivery<br>Competitive price<br>Consistent quality<br>Uncompromising service<br>Brand name recognition | Customer satisfaction |
| Robust design | Consistent quality |
| Statistical quality control<br>Six Sigma and/or ppm<br>Design of experiments<br>Analysis of variance<br>Statistical process control | Robust design |
| Process inputs (5Ms and an E) | Statistical process control |
| Conveyer speed<br>Operating temperature<br>Operator skill level<br>Humidity level<br>Measurement capability | Process inputs (5Ms and an E) |

## PERFORMANCE MEASUREMENTS & METRICS EXAMPLE

Baseball is a game that includes players with assigned positions and roles who additionally paintings collectively on a extra team. Baseball is one manner to demonstrate how agencies can use numerous performance measurements or performance metrics to assess the fulfillment or failure of people, as well as their teams.

Pitchers are frequently evaluated through their earned run average (ERA), their total number of strikeouts, and the number of hits they yield. For instance, ERA is the quantity of runs scored towards a tumbler consistent with 9 innings pitched. An ERA of 2.05 indicates that for multiple video games, a pitcher had 2.05 runs scored against him or her for each nine innings pitched.

Position gamers are frequently evaluated on both offensive and protective abilities.

Offensively, a position participant is rated on his or her hitting talents, consisting of batting common (BA), runs batted in (RBI), and on-base percent (OBP). BA is the variety of hits in keeping with quantity of instances at bat. A BA of .400 is exquisite, but not often achieved. A BA of. Three hundred is right. A BA of. One hundred is typical of maximum pitchers, who aren't normally considered professional hitters.

Defensively, a role participant is ranked in step with fielding percent (FP), or the potential to seize and throw a ball without committing an mistakes. This consists of catching a batted ball and securing an out, throwing the ball to the proper base to secure a putout, or making an accurate throw to the proper base. FP is the variety of fielding opportunities performed without a mistakes divided via the full range of possibilities.

# Chapter 5: Customer Focus and Market Positioning

Understanding consumer needs is an essential part of any enterprise. By knowing what your clients want, you can better tailor almost each aspect of your business, specially your advertising approach. In this newsletter, we speak what client desires are, along with the way to recognize your customers' needs.

**What are client needs?**
Customer wishes are the incentive behind a patron's selection-making technique. The consumer's choice is what drives them to purchase a product and to pick out that product over every other. Businesses examine their customers' wishes to offer higher products, advertising and marketing techniques and customer service.

**Types of purchaser wishes**
There are basically sorts of customer needs: bodily and psychological. These needs regularly overlap, which now and again makes it challenging to split them. Physical desires are the simplest to pick out, as they

regularly have direct answers. For example, if someone is hungry, they want something to consume.

Psychological wishes are occasionally harder to identify; however, they are also commonly the extra effective motive force of patron decisions. For example, even as a physical want tells a consumer they need something to consume, a mental need directs them in the direction of meals that gives them with a selected feeling. Psychological wishes can be the distinction between a client buying a salad over a burger due to the fact they need to experience healthful.

To better apprehend the customers' desires, do not forget each their bodily and mental wishes. Some commonplace sorts of client need encompass:

**Price:** A product that fits into their non-public budget

**Experience:** An exciting enjoy while using the product

**Function:** A product that solves a particular trouble for the purchaser

**Feeling:** A unique feeling the patron will have at the same time as the usage of your product

Compatibility: A product that works well with the alternative merchandise your consumer makes use of

**Personal:** A non-public enjoy the consumer has while interacting with a brand or contacting customer service

Social: A product that incorporates social reputation, inclusive of shopping for the trendy version vehicle to electrify coworkers

## How to recognize your clients' wishes?

A thorough information of your customers' wishes requires evaluation. Here are 4 steps you may observe to apprehend your clients' desires and flip this records into actionable consequences:

### 1. Create a consumer's personality

To apprehend your customers' desires, you want to first recognize who your consumer is. You can start through crafting a client character, that is a fictional description of your best client, based on studies and your modern patron base. It describes the sort of character your enterprise appeals to, inclusive of their possibly age, gender, place, income and interests.

With an in depth customer personality, you may reflect on consideration on the needs of that audience. For example, a audience of women in their 50s may additionally have exclusive desires than men of their 20s. A consumer character helps you keep your ideal purchaser in mind as you are gaining knowledge of and defining their wishes in later stages.

**2. Seek remarks out of your customers**
One of the first-class ways to understand your clients' needs is by using getting remarks from them without delay. You can ask clients what they like about your products, what they dislike and what they would like to look changed. There are numerous methods to do this, like sending out surveys, maintaining attention groups and tracking discussions across social media.

When asking for feedback out of your clients, don't forget to invite a huge variety of questions. Try to study more about each their physical and psychological wishes. Ask them about how the product made them feel, along with their revel in physically the use of the product.

As you gather this comments, collect all of the effects and enforce the advised adjustments. You can then go again in your clients and spot if the changes improved them enjoy. This manner of gathering comments, implementing modifications and reassessing is critical for now not only understanding purchaser wishes however for making appropriate use of the information you obtain.

**3. Analyze your competitors**

Your competitors also play a position in figuring out your clients' needs and wants. If one of your important competitors offers a brand new carrier or function, your target audience will come to assume this in all their buying alternatives. For example, if a software enterprise that gives a product similar to your own gives a 30-day loose trial, your target audience can also count on the equal from you.

You can examine your competition in addition as you accumulated remarks from your clients. Conduct attention companies wherein you show the two products aspect by means of facet, keep interviews with customers of the opposite commercial enterprise and track their social mentions. From this, you may learn how your competition is assembly the desires of your audience and how they could improve, which you could then use to enhance your merchandise.

**4. Craft a customer needs declaration**

With a customer wishes announcement, you're defining the precise needs of your target audience and putting them into one succinct declaration. Use the data you amassed within the preceding steps to inform the content material of your patron desires announcement.

To craft a useful customer needs declaration, there are some factors to goal for:

Consistency: Aim for a declaration that stays steady over time. Your consumer's personality is the identical throughout the product development process, so your declaration must be as nicely. Keeping a consistent needs announcement guarantees you may set up strategies for reaching the ones needs.

Usefulness to the patron: Your wishes assertion ought to describe how your product will meet a purchaser's desires better than a competitor. Use the records you collected approximately your opposition to describe what you could do higher than them.

Usefulness on your commercial enterprise: Create a wishes statement which can assist out each department to your corporation. From this assertion your advertising team need to know the pleasant way to promote a product, the product improvement team ought to understand what upgrades to make and the sales group should recognize a way to first-rate sell the product.

Clearness and conciseness: Everyone who reads this announcement must recognize exactly what it's far your clients are looking for. Keep the language easy and correct for the quality outcomes.

## 10 Strategies for enhancing customer experience

Not most effective can a fine revel in help brands interact with present customers, however it may additionally assist agencies stand proud of competitors. By fostering a first-rate CX, organizations can improve sales thru retention and growth consumer lifetime value.

As the search for customers keeps to characteristic more competition, brands are searching out new ways to create connections and meet ever-rising expectancies. Here are 10 approaches to enhance the customer enjoy to your emblem in nowadays market.

## 1. Listen for your client

While it is able to seem obvious, many manufacturers forget the importance of client feedback. When seeking out new approaches to enhance CX, look no similarly than the clients themselves. Their comments can provide ample perception so long as organizations take a look at in with them frequently and in approaches that support measurement and accountability.

With nowadays generation stacks, leaders have many approaches they could attain out to customers and capitalize on remarks. Some of the most commonplace consist of surveys, which ask precise questions about stories, services, and products to determine what customers really think about a emblem and their engagement with it. The timeliest use of surveys is to send one thru e mail after a particular interaction.

For real-time remarks, manufacturers also can turn to alternatives together with chat and social media. Companies can inspire clients to percentage their tales and experiences concerning new products, carrier interactions, or even the new ideas they would like to see a brand deliver to marketplace next.

Leaders can also consider enforcing a voice of the customer (VoC) application. This creates a greater formal framework to collect customer comments, honing in on preferences and expectations round particular products or service traces. The input from those packages is used to assist corporations increase new services at the same time as making sure issues and proceedings are addressed to avoid additional effect. Most VoC tasks are tied to business goals to form development plans, realign customer support strategies, and improve advertising and marketing efforts.

## 2. Understand your customer

Taking what you found out from paying attention to customers and reading it from a business attitude can create a deeper knowledge of target segmentations and buyer personas. Leaders must take the feedback they collect and leverage analytical equipment to higher recognize their behavior and the way it is able to be used to further refine commercial enterprise operations and goals.

Some of this information takes the form of demographics and better insight into the target audience. This may want to consist of age, vicinity, gender, buy history, and more. Data may be used to discover developments and discover what's and isn't resonating with specific buyers.

This information may additionally result in some key insights, together with new or distinctive client personas that want to be broken out and addressed to make certain that messaging resonates throughout all consumer sorts. It can also permit for greater personalization in messaging and customer service, which clients have come to assume. In fact, 73% of clients expect brands to recognize their expectations.

## 3. Map your consumer's adventure

At an excessive degree, a patron journey is the total of the interactions a client has with a brand, whether thru direct touch or indirect evaluate. For leaders to ensure fine CX, they need to apprehend the stairs an individual takes from prospect to real client. This includes listing out and studying all of the one of a kind touchpoint, pain points, and moves that effect the buying decision.

Here are only some ways that mapping and know-how the consumer's journey can assist enhance their impression of an emblem:

Reduce friction. Identify degrees in which consumers fail to move ahead with a buy choice and do away with any hurdles to make the shopping for process greater seamless.

Optimize touchpoints. Consider the points where customers interact — or fail to have interaction — with content material, after which refine messaging to better resonate for acquisition and retention.

Provide seamless customer service. Consolidate advertising and customer service messaging to prioritize communications. Leaders can use gear to streamline guide to align with the consumer lifecycle to provide the proper statistics on the right time.

**4. Hire and broaden a sturdy crew**

Quality trumps quantity when it comes to assembling a strong CX team, that may embody the entirety from advertising to assist. Businesses can usually grow their groups to scale to call for. But having a strong foundation of a team that is nicely-skilled on the necessities of a business — including each products and way of life — can pass a long manner to ensuring customer pleasure.

Make sure to provide all group members with education not simply at the fundamentals of how services and products work but also how the emblem as an entire expects customers to be dealt with. Whether they name in with a question or a grievance, bear in mind the client's perspective and guide personnel to be hassle-solvers instead of just trying to push via a fixed quantity of calls, emails, or chat discussions every day.

### 5. Listen for your team

Leaders also can examine plenty from the folks who are at the frontlines of client interactions. Be positive to acquire feedback now not simply from clients however additionally from customer service groups. These are the corporations of individuals who are managing customers firsthand and can help leaders pick out areas for development or styles in patron conduct really worth addressing to improve the client revel in.

There are different delivered benefits that come from being attentive to current employees. Consider that 80% of staff contributors who sense preferred and heard paintings more difficult in the long time. In turn, this can have an immediate effect on the first-class of client studies organizations are capable of offer. In contrast, 34% of personnel are probable to depart a task in the event that they don't sense valued or diagnosed.

### 6. Deliver exquisite customer support

Understanding a customer base and building a robust group are foundational to having superb customer support, which regularly stands on the crossroads of wonderful or bad CX. Half of all purchasers will depart a emblem in the event that they have a terrible customer service stumble upon, although they were previously loyal to that employer.

Creating a consumer-centric subculture at the same time as setting the proper employees within the proper region at the proper time can move a protracted manner in the direction of supporting deliver top-quality provider. Brands also can take advantage of tools to assist their customer service teams be extra effective, green, and on challenge. Live chat helps many groups reduce down the time it takes for customers to receive assist and improve first-contact resolution. Self-carrier portals, understanding bases, and videos also can permit clients help themselves in lieu of or even as they look forward to extra help.

## 7. Connect along with your clients

Many client interactions with a brand are inbound. The consumer has a question or trouble and wishes recommendation or a decision to remain thrilled with the product or service. But corporations also can be proactive with their outbound messaging and create connections with customers that enhance engagement and loyalty whilst enhancing CX.

Keep all messaging, reactive or in any other case, clear and concise so clients can discover what they need and retain on their way. This includes help articles and account get right of entry to proper along emblem content and promotions. Maintain messaging this is patron-centric and relatable, putting the focus at the purchaser experience and outcomes beyond natural income. The right messaging can also create an emotional connection with the patron, assisting to underscore loyalty and empathy that locations a logo in a effective mild.

**8. Take an Omni channel approach**
The customer adventure won't be as linear as marketers or enterprise operators prefer. Instead, take into account the one-of-a-kind channels a consumer uses to have interaction with a emblem. From web sites, social structures, emails, hotlines, or even brick-and-

mortar locations, clients are Omni channel, this means that CX wishes to recollect this method as properly.

Companies can gain from retaining their logo voice consistent across extraordinary marketing and contact channels. When a client feels that a whole crew is on the identical page, it is able to assist them appreciate the experience even extra. In reality, 90% of clients expect a constant experience with a brand, regardless of the channel they pick out to connect via.

And for those worried that an Omni channel approach ought to create silos across internal operations, equipment are the answer. Project management, content material control, and patron courting control platforms can deliver every person together in a unmarried region.

**9. Tap into synthetic intelligence**

It may appear like a buzzword; however, AI is here to live. More than three-quarters of companies are engaged with AI already, and a Gartner take a look at discovered that undertaking capital corporations have invested extra than $1.7 billion in generative AI. Most prominently, AI enables the usage of catboats that guide customer support, allowing brands to offer quicker and around-the-clock aid at the same time as additionally automating responses with more personalized content.

Of direction, AI need to now not absolutely update human intervention in customer service. But it can empower current personnel to perform extra correctly and successfully. Tools can provide caused content, automation, and optimization while making ready customer service sellers to exactly cope with client issues. There also are software packages that could check which content plays excellent to allow leaders to curate the purchaser adventure based on what clicks with a target market.

**10. Create metrics and song ROI**

Most corporations have no scarcity of analytics and reporting equipment to decide business goals and outline success. But many brands forget key metrics tied without delay to the customer experience as a hallmark of commercial enterprise health and boom. When it involves monitoring CX drivers, including Net Promoter Score, best 15% of leaders said the manner their business enterprise became measuring CX turned into fully excellent. Monitoring CX drivers can be one of the most crucial metrics for a agency that is suffering to preserve clients or supply tremendous purchaser reviews.

Other CX metrics leaders can explore encompass social media reach, shares, and impressions. This can suggest how engaged a customer base is with a given services or products presenting. Time spent on a internet site or critical webpages also can be telling concerning what's resonating with customers.

The metrics a organization makes a decision to degree must in the end be tied to the dreams set. But with out monitoring progress in opposition to those targeted accomplishments, leaders could have problem defining with truth whether or not they're offering a excellent patron revel in.

## Mastering Brand Differentiation and Positioning Strategy

Positioning is the area within the marketplace you want your commercial enterprise to hold, mainly within the mind's eye of your target market. It may be diffused and hard to come across but may be less difficult to spot in case you look at it out of your personal function as a purchaser. Take vehicles, for example, in which the concept of notion as truth excels. BMW and Mercedes Benz function themselves as luxury vehicles, Tesla sets itself aside as a easy electricity opportunity, and Kia and Hyundai logo themselves as low priced.

What function should your offerings occupy to your capacity consumer's mind? How do you need people to think about you? Influencing perception (who you are, the way you help, what you may uniquely do for a consumer) are what positioning is all approximately.

**What is Differentiation?**

Differentiation relates to positioning within the sense you want to attract the identical customers your opposition attracts. If another expert services company's offerings overlap with your target audience, you want to think about the way you'll stand out and be the extra appealing option.

A commonplace false impression is that being inexpensive than the competition is the first-class manner to distinguish your self. We'll get into that a touch more later, however it's secure to say that's typically a very good way to end up in a race to the lowest.

To understand why most different a success brands don't critically underneath-fee their merchandise or carrier, positioned yourself in the customer role again. When you're within the mood for a smooth drink, do you choose Pepsi, Coke, Sprite, or another famous brand? Why do you choose it? Is it for the taste, the level of caffeine, or is something extra intangible like the correct reminiscences it conjures up? These traits are what differentiate one gentle drink from the subsequent.

Let's observe a selected example of Nike's positioning method. Nike provides a commodity object (shoes) to masses of millions of humans around the sector each year. Nike is horizontally located. Their position is they trust in 'celebrating the excessive acting athlete in you' – whether the client is a real athlete or not, they attraction to that demographic. They returned this role up with 'merchandise which can be sturdy, bendy and light-weight that will help you push further and faster than ever before to 'win'. They simply manifest to make footwear.

Shoes, at the floor, are all tons the equal. But regular, lots of humans choose Nike – due to the fact Nike embodies that position in their thoughts.

### The Differentiation/Positioning Connection

Positioning and differentiation connect in essential approaches. It can be difficult, but a great way to examine it's far:

Positioning is based on the differentiating characteristics or qualities that make your enterprise better than your competition's inside the thoughts of your target market.

Both concepts are strategic actions and are designed to create a favored role in your business inside the market in place of having or not it's defined by your competition. The result is your ideal customers have a compelling motive to select you.

To illustrate our positioning and differentiation points on this piece, we'll use an accounting organization as an instance. The principles blanketed, although, follow to whichever expert service quarter you're in.

**What's a Brand Differentiation Strategy?**
Here's a reasonably easy manner to illustrate a differentiation approach. A professional service organization such as an accounting organization can **have a vertical or horizontal function. What does that imply?**

Vertical segmentation is industry or category unique. Your attention on operating with customers in a particular field – such as health care, facts technology, or tour organizations and many others. For example, an accounting firm may work specifically with clients in the creation industry.

Horizontal segmentation takes into consideration demographic information or the specialty you hold. So, one accounting firm may best paintings with excessive-well worth individuals or households. Clients may come from many sectors, however they've a selected trait in not unusual.

It's additionally possible to mix the 2. For instance, a forensic accountant (horizontal) handiest works in the creation area (vertical) or an property and accept as true with accounting company (horizontal) handiest works with people bringing in more than one million a 12 months (additionally horizontal).

**Planning Your Brand Differentiation Strategy**

To get commenced strategizing how your corporation will differentiate itself, examine how you currently deal with your enterprise model. Does your phase usually invoice through the hour? Is the target market you want to attain no longer mainly interested in looking their bill climb with each smartphone name, electronic mail, or other hobby? If so, you might want to layout a brand new commercial enterprise model in which you rate a retainer and the relaxation is billed as a percentage of outcomes.

Before we circulate directly to the different types of differentiation strategies, allows recap:

Positioning is the region you keep within the mind's eye of your audience.

Differentiation is how your organization is different or stands proud out of your competition on a non-price foundation.

From a advertising and marketing angle this is crucial, especially for expert carrier groups whose common customer won't realize especially what the company does. Put every other manner, pretty plenty absolutely everyone is aware of what an accountant does, however they don't recognize the bits and bobs of unique offerings.

Your ability to connect with an audience rests on positioning and differentiation. If the manner you gift yourself and your offerings relates to people on a one-to-one foundation, the more likely it's miles they'll feel emotionally linked along with your firm and do business with it.

## Types of Brand Differentiation Strategies

A differentiation strategy is multi-pronged however can typically be condensed into 3 steps:

Identifying differentiating competitive advantages.
Choosing the aggressive blessings in order to build the excellent position.
Selecting a global positioning method.
Once finished, you have to then correctly talk your preferred function to the market.

The proper positioning method improves your brand's visibility both on-line and in the minds of your target market. There are numerous procedures you could take and, as we mentioned earlier than, not often if ever is decreasing your fee certainly one of them.

**Here's what we recommend alternatively:**

What functions of your provider may be highlighted that differentiate you out of your competitors? What do you want to be known for?

What benefits does your carrier offer that the competition does not?

What precise troubles does your target audience have that most effective you could remedy?

How do your services financially advantage clients in the event that they act these days?
Are there additional offerings or capabilities you may offer including get entry to complementary service firms?

Whatever it takes to make your organization stand out—and as lengthy as it gives actual price—is what defines a great differentiation approach.

**How to Choose a Brand Differentiation Strategy?**
It frequently takes place you'll want to choose between two similarly placed options. That's wherein differentiation helps inside the choice-making manner. For example, at the surface the percentages are suitable that accounting corporations can meet comparable needs of a centered marketplace phase. The

differentiation questions set out above assist you drill right down to discover why your organization is the only they should pick out.

What you're trying to do is lay out qualitative, focused, and innovative traits that disrupt or trade the norm of ways people do business along with your kind of expert service.

With product differentiation, it could be less difficult due to the fact manufacturers can provide you with unique functions that set them apart. With expert services, a variety of the work is finished on a one-to-one foundation to fulfill a customer's desires, so one suitable way to differentiate is in the way your marketplace and "sell" your offerings. It's approximately supplying fee earlier than they even emerge as a customer.

**Case in point:**

An ordinary digital advertising and marketing approach for accountants and other carrier providers is going something like this: Here's a listing of our offerings, here is what we provide to cope with your hassle, might you like to lease us? please join up the dotted line.

You would possibly differentiate yourself via making the method greater consultative. For instance, when a ability client first speaks to someone for your company, that character may stroll them thru a unique procedure to assist them understand in which they are of their journey, wherein they want to be, and the stairs your firm is going to take them via to get there. With this method, even if the offerings you offer are precisely what a competing organization gives, the manner you sell them can be a great differentiating approach to try.

Or try innovating inside the provider itself. Can you turn up your commercial enterprise version, reconfigure the structure you comply with, and add in more services you provide but others don't? Explain to ability clients why those services, say like a particular piece of software program or proprietary tech, will accelerate the process. Selling that experience makes your offerings that rather more compelling.

## What Makes You So Special?

Do you presently have a differentiation method? Is it running? How do you know?

## Here's some methods you may determine it:

First and fundamental, how laser-centered do you seem from your target audience's angle? Many professional services enterprise proprietors fall into the catch 22 situation of being too close to the situation. They understand all of the internal workings of the enterprise, which includes things a client never thinks approximately. You would possibly say you simply undeniable realize too much. And understanding an excessive amount of can get for your manner of connecting with a potential consumer. Ask yourself rather, what does the capability client see when they check out your enterprise?

What's the message your professional service business enterprise is placing out there? Is it clear via your advertising what the vertical, horizontal, or mixture function is you keep in the marketplace?

Are you successfully communicating your differentiation through charge, pleasant, and awareness? Is the message being made clean? Is it regular in each single channel you operate, i.e. Does the heading in your website's domestic page say the equal factor as your organization's brochure? Is your middle message communicated through all social media systems?

Does the stuff you write approximately in your blog continually relate again to your particular position?

In the cease, differentiating and positioning yourself in a prevailing way is set searching at your market as a whole. To pull out in the front of your competitors, put yourself in the footwear of ability customers, look at what the opposition is doing, and devise a listing of what you can offer that units you apart.

Not seeing a good deal to set you firm aside from the others? Here's the deal, if all and sundry for your line of work or niche is offering the exact same things, no person is positioning or differentiating themselves. If you all have the equal service list, if all of it appears the same from outside, chances are it is all the identical. So even in case you assume your offerings are higher, the manner your marketplace your self-gained rely if absolutely everyone else is doing it the exact same way.

Today, most business relationships start online. If a capability purchaser can't tell from looking at your internet site how you're one of a kind or if they could handiest understand your differentiation through talking to a personnel member, then it's not working. Customers nowadays don't want to spend time "studying you" once they're in your office or on an internet session. Want to construct patron satisfaction and loyalty? Give them the entirety they want to know about you ahead of time.

One of the biggest payoffs you'll understand from this approach is that you'll recognize you stand a very good danger of maintaining the customer due to the fact they've already vetted you. They're satisfied due to the fact they don't waste time locating out you can't provide them what they need and you're happy because you haven't spent in any other case effective time on a potential patron who's no longer a great in shape.

One very last tip. When defining your differentiators keep away from cliché phrases and terms like nice, quality effects, and professional communicators. "We're extremely good expert" isn't the right answer to what makes you special!

The bottom line: if you could respond "absolutely everyone" when asked who you serve, you're now not well-sufficient placed within the market. In truth, you're now not placed at all. It's time to get to paintings building a differentiation strategy that improves your business' visibility and gives you the aggressive gain you deserve.

## Conclusion

In end, "Mastering Business Excellence: Secrets to Win in Today's Market" has journeyed thru the critical factors of reaching and maintaining excellence in cutting-edge business environments. From expertise the dynamic competitive landscape to embracing strategic imaginative and prescient and making plans, each bankruptcy has delved into important aspects consisting of leadership, operational efficiency, client centricity, innovation, sustainability, financial control, advertising prowess, and global enlargement techniques. By synthesizing ancient insights with contemporary exceptional practices, this e book equips commercial enterprise leaders with actionable techniques to navigate complexities, foster non-stop improvement, and capitalize on rising possibilities. As we look ahead, gaining knowledge of commercial enterprise excellence not handiest complements organizational overall performance however additionally fosters resilience in navigating the ever-evolving global market terrain, ensuring sustained achievement inside the years yet to come.

www.ingramcontent.com/pod-product-compliance
Lightning Source LLC
Chambersburg PA
CBHW071922210526
45479CB00002B/515